Latina/o Communication Studies

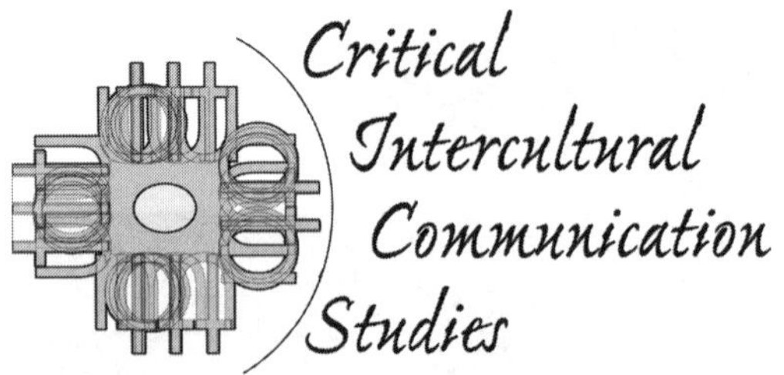

Critical
Intercultural
Communication
Studies

Thomas K. Nakayama
General Editor

Vol. 9

PETER LANG
New York • Washington, D.C./Baltimore • Bern
Frankfurt am Main • Berlin • Brussels • Vienna • Oxford

Bernadette Marie Calafell

Latina/o Communication Studies

Theorizing Performance

PETER LANG
New York • Washington, D.C./Baltimore • Bern
Frankfurt am Main • Berlin • Brussels • Vienna • Oxford

Library of Congress Cataloging-in-Publication Data

Calafell, Bernadette Marie.
Latina/o communication studies: theorizing performance / Bernadette Marie Calafell.
p. cm. — (Critical intercultural communication studies; v. 9)
Includes bibliographical references.
1. Hispanic Americans—Ethnic identity. 2. Hispanic Americans—
Study and teaching (Higher). 3. Hispanic American women—Social conditions.
4. Hispanic American men—Social conditions. 5. Intercultural communication—
United States. 6. Interpersonal communication—United States. 7. Power (Social sciences)—
United States. 8. Performative (Philosophy)—Social aspects—United States.
9. Performance art—Social aspects—United States. 10. United States—Ethnic relations.
I. Title. II. Title: Latina communication studies. III. Title: Latino communication studies.
E184.S75C347   973'.0468—dc22   2007035022
ISBN 978-0-8204-8182-1
ISSN 1528-6118

Bibliographic information published by **Die Deutsche Bibliothek**.
Die Deutsche Bibliothek lists this publication in the "Deutsche
Nationalbibliografie"; detailed bibliographic data is available
on the Internet at http://dnb.ddb.de/.

Cover design by Joni Holst
Cover image: *Listening,* © 2003 by María DeGuzmán,
Camera Query. www.cameraquery.com

The paper in this book meets the guidelines for permanence and durability
of the Committee on Production Guidelines for Book Longevity
of the Council of Library Resources.

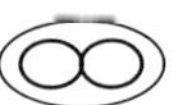

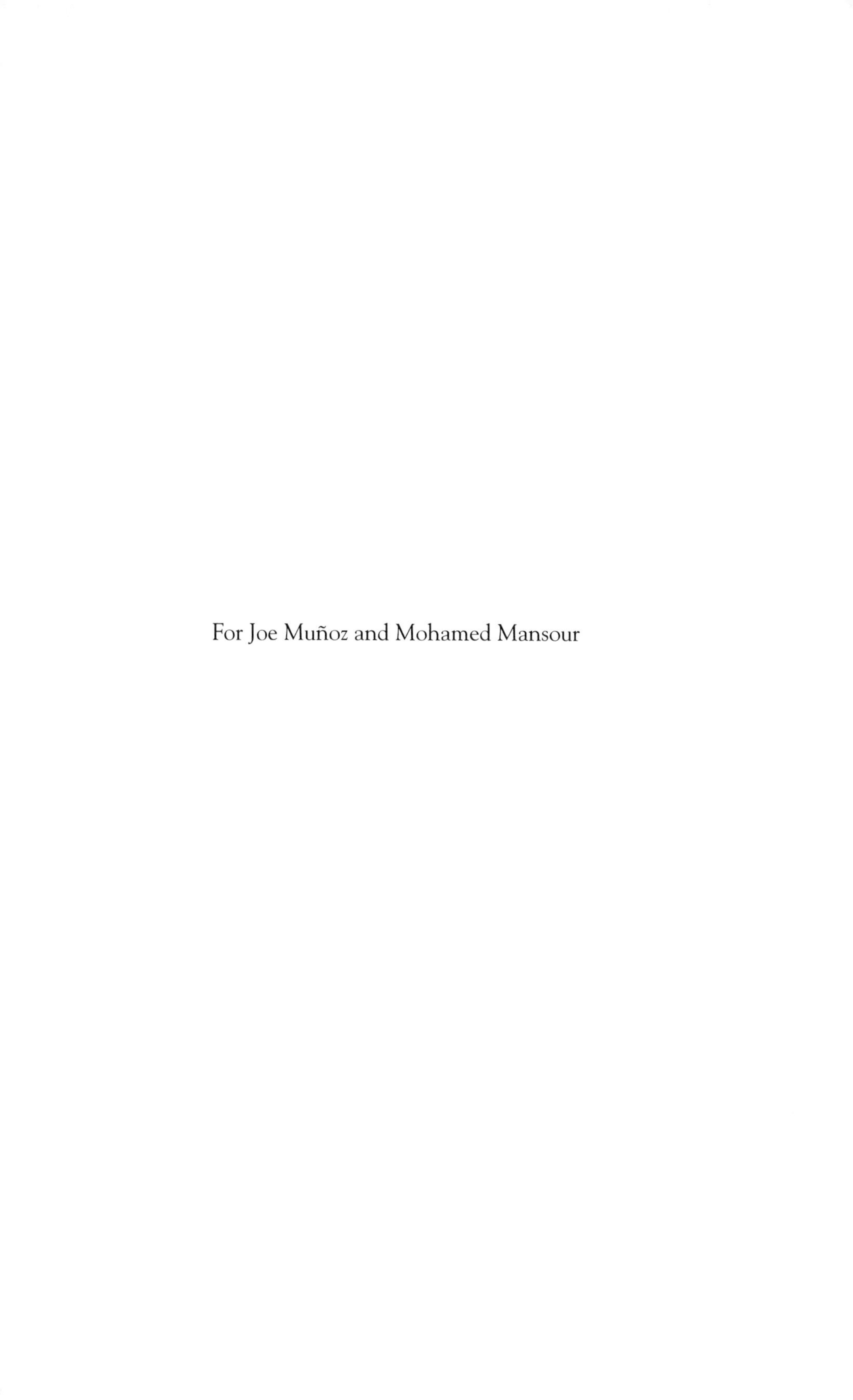

For Joe Muñoz and Mohamed Mansour

TABLE OF CONTENTS

ACKNOWLEDGMENTS

There are several people who have been instrumental in supporting me and this project throughout its various manifestations.

I first want to thank D. Soyini Madison for being a wonderfully supportive and caring advisor and friend both during and after my time at the University of North Carolina at Chapel Hill. She as well as Della Pollock, Maria DeGuzman, Robert J. Cox, and Rich Cante challenged me to think about performance, identity, queerness, and memory in new ways.

Fernando Delgado, thank you for being a consistent and caring mentor who continues to offer me insight, inspiration, and support. Your presence in my life has been invaluable in ways you cannot even imagine.

Frederick Corey, thank you for introducing me to the world of Performance Studies and forever changing me both personally and professionally. You let me know that my voice mattered, and for that I am eternally grateful. Like Fred, Kristin Valentine, Sarah Amira de la Garza, and Olga Davis were central in my early understandings of performance and ethnography and I thank them for all they taught me.

I would also like to thank Michelle Holling and Lisa Flores for their continual support as I have moved from undergraduate student to faculty member. Your guidance, friendship, and research have been central to my coming to find my place in this space.

I would like to thank Tom Nakayama, not only as the series editor, but as a teacher, mentor, and friend.

Thank you to my colleagues and friends at the University of Denver, particularly those in the Department of Human Communication and the Center for Multicultural Excellence.

At Syracuse University I received emotional support and friendship from Diane Grimes, Sandra Faulkner, Joshua Atkinson, and Linda Martín Alcoff at a time when I needed it the most. Thank you so much.

I could not have finished this project, or any project for that matter, without the loving friendships of Lisa Calvente and Shane Moreman. Each of you has continued to challenge me personally and professionally, pushing me in all my endeavors to strive for excellence. I only hope I can offer you as much as you have given me.

I would also like to thank my graduate student cohorts at both Arizona State University and the University of North Carolina at Chapel Hill, including Phaedra Pezzullo, Nina Reich, Rachel Hall, Rivka Eisner, James Cahill, Nathan Epley, Robb Romanowski. P. Michael Mackey, Christina Foust, Kate Willink, C. Wesley Buerkle, Raquel Monroe, and Naida Zukic.

I would like to thank my students at Arizona State University, the University of North Carolina at Chapel Hill, Syracuse University, and the University of Denver for all your inspiration, support, and challenges to make me a better teacher and researcher.

I would also like to thank Angharad Valdivia and Michael Bowman for publishing previous versions of Chapters 2 and 3. Thank you to Taylor and Francis for granting permission to reprint previously published essays that appear here in extended form: Calafell, Bernadette Marie. "Pro(re-)claiming Loss: A Performative Pilgrimage in Search of Malintzin Tenépal." *Text and Performance Quarterly* 25 (2005): 43–56. Calafell, Bernadette Marie. "Disrupting the Dichotomy: 'Yo Soy Chicana/o?' in the New Latina/o South." *The Communication Review* 7 (2004):175–204. In addition, I would like to thank Tes Thraves for allowing me to include the photograph of me in my street performance. Thanks to Maria DeGuzman for the use of her artwork for the cover of this book. *Listening* © 2003 by María DeGuzmán, Camera Query. www.cameraquery.com.

Finally, I would like to thank both my mother, Martha Muñoz, and my partner, Mohamed Mansour, for their unconditional support and love.

· 1 ·

MAKING A SPACE FOR LATINA/O PERFORMANCE

I have been thinking about Latina/o performance for quite some time, even before I knew that the object of my affection was performance. I watched my family members, especially my grandparents, move in and out of identities and speech patterns depending on which space we were in. At home, in South Phoenix, in our mostly Mexican, Chicana/o, and African American neighborhood, they seemed at ease and often spoke in English, Spanish, and Spanglish. Outside South Phoenix, I saw more formal presentations of the self, as if they were aware of an audience, often one with more power. Their performances were not disingenuous, based in deception; rather, they understood issues of power, race, class, and gender and how each space was a site to be negotiated and navigated carefully.

As I grew older, I too found myself engaged in performance, though not fully aware of the politics behind the performance. I moved between Mexican, Hispanic, Mexican American, Chicana, and Latina as I sought to make connections and negotiate my sense of self in various spaces. Each of these identities meant something unique, with varying ideologies and, for me, identifications that changed over time. In the choices permitted by these labels I was in a sense performing affiliation, accommodation, assimilation, and resistance. Each of these labels was a performative option right before me, even if I did not fully comprehend that what I was doing was choosing to strategically perform an identity.

After joining a master's program in communication studies, I became intrigued by the possibility of theorizing and mapping Latina/o performance. I wanted to understand how power, resistance, and identity all played into the conscious and unconscious choices made by my grandparents and myself. However, I found that within the field of communication studies, Latina/o studies, let alone Latina/o performance, was largely ignored and underdeveloped. Sadly this is not a new or surprising situation, as Latina/os are often simply glossed over and ignored by the hegemonic black and white binary into which we do not fit easily as mixed-raced peoples (Alcoff).

I was, however, introduced to the scholarship of others outside my field, in drama, theater, performance art, and performance studies, such as Coco Fusco, Alberto Sandoval-Sánchez, and José Esteban Muñoz. I found their work to be useful and important, but these scholars did not always ask the questions that I felt were central to the line of inquiry I wanted to pursue. Madison and Hamera write of performance as a contested concept that is fundamental to life and culture. They argue, "We enter the everyday and the ordinary and interpret its symbolic universe to discover the complexities of its extraordinary meanings and practices" (xii). Part of their framing performance in this way connects to discussions of identity and perfomativity. In thinking through the work I present here and my larger research plan, I would never specifically claim to be an expert on performativity or even to understand all its various theoretical manifestations, but I do believe its base form guides much of my work. Madison and Hamera provide an excellent overview of various approaches to performativity, ranging from Butler's citational perspective, which highlights how identity categories are socially constructed, to performativity as resistance or intervention against citationality (xviii–xix). Performativity becomes "the interconnected triad of identity, experience, and social relations—encompassing the admixture of class, race, sex, geography, religion" (xix). Madison and Hamera pose the question, "When we rework performativity beyond a 'stylized repetition of acts' into the more deeply evocation of performativity as 'nonessentialized constructions of identity,' what does it then actually look like?" (xix). They argue that in the layering of performatives within cultural performances, performatives are "doubly layered with a difference: they are re-presented, re-located, and re-materialized for possibility of a substantial reconsideration and re-examination" (xix). Madison and Hamera's presentation of performativity is the crux of how I wanted to engage with the study of performance and Latina/o studies. It is at the center of this book.

The paucity of work that addressed Latina/o performance taking this approach in communication studies contributed to my lack of a disciplinary identity. Thus, it has become my desire to contribute to the formation of Latina/o performance within communication studies. In undertaking this task, I first map the terrain of Latina/o communication studies to make the argument for the development of a Latina/o performance studies project. I then briefly describe my approach to the study of performance and identity, which moves beyond this initial discussion of performativity. Finally, I offer an overview of this text.

Latina/o Communication Studies

As an undergraduate, my first encounter with Latina/os in the field of communication came in a methods course in which we were assigned to read an essay by Lisa Flores titled "Creating Discursive Space through a Rhetoric of Difference: Chicana Feminists Craft a Homeland." While the essay became extremely important to me at that time as the first piece of research in communication (and, frankly, in my college experience) that spoke to my experiences and identities, I had no idea just how significant it would become to me as I entered graduate school. Flores' essay not only introduced me to the very real possibility of studying Chicana identities in the academy but also shaped and demonstrated to me the most dominant tradition used to study Latina/o communication—rhetorical criticism or textual analysis. As a scholar in training I adopted a rhetorical perspective, initially resisting performance. However, as I became more enmeshed in the work, I came to see what I believe to be a false split between rhetoric and performance. In taking a critical humanistic approach in this text, I center my overview on rhetorical scholarship focusing on Latina/os and the emerging performance work because of what I believe to be a symbiotic relationship between the two that has largely been ignored. My hope is that this text will challenge this split by creating a more complex and less Eurocentric understanding of rhetoric.

In examining the emergence of Latina/o studies in the field of communication we can see how rhetorical scholars contributed to scholarship in social movements and protest rhetoric by analyzing the speeches and texts produced by male rhetors of the Chicano movement, such as César

Chávez, Corky Gonzales, Reijes Tijerina, and José Angel Gutíerrez (Delgado "Chicano Movement Rhetoric"; Jensen and Hammerback; Hammerback and Jensen "The Rhetorical Worlds of César Chávez," "No Revolution without Poets," "Ethnic Heritage As Rhetorical Legacy," *The Rhetorical Career of César Chávez*; Fernandez and Jensen; Sedano). In addition to these studies of the movement rhetoric, Flores and Hasian examined vernacular discourses produced in Chicana/o newspapers. In more recent years we have seen studies examining both Puerto Rican and Nuyorican rhetorics of protest (Cordova; Enck-Wanzer), as well as the rhetorics of international figures such as Rigoberta Menchú (Delgado "Rigoberta Menchú") and Fidel Castro (Delgado "The Rhetoric of Fidel Castro"). Flores examined the literature produced by Chicana feminists in order to chart the strategies by which they create discursive space and make bridges with potential allies ("Creating Discursive Space"), and González identified rhetorics of Otherness ("Mexican Otherness").

More recently, scholars have turned to examining visual rhetorics (LaWare; Calafell and Delgado), masculinity (Delgado "All along the Border", "Golden but Not Brown"; Delgado and Calafell; Holling "*El Simpatic* Boxer"), and immigration (Calafell "Performing the Responsible Sponsor"; Flores "Constructing Rhetorical Borders"). Popular culture, including film and television (Flores "Challenging the Myth"; Valdivia), the Internet (Holling "Forming Oppositional"), music (Delgado "Chicano Ideology Revisited"), and magazines (Calafell "In Our Own Image"; Delgado "When the Silenced Speak"), remained a prominent area of study. In addition, an increasing number of studies examined the media constructions of Latina/o celebrities, including Jennifer Lopez (Beltrán) and Selena (Willis and González; González and Willis).

Taking more qualitative or interpretative approaches, de la Garza critically examines her life as a Chicana through auto/ethnography and staged performance, while Martinez assumes a phenomenological stance to do the same. The most recent area of study of Latina/os and communication has been within the realm of performance. Though one could make the argument that previous studies, including some cited above, have engaged issues of performance, I mark the following studies as naming performance as being central to method (i.e., performance ethnography, staged performance), presentation (performative writing), theory, and text. Menchaca offers an autoethnographic performance centering on the image of the Virgin of Guadalupe. Likewise, in my own work I document my performance pilgrimage in search of La Malinche/Malintzin Tenépal, the translator of Hernan Cortés (Calafell, "Pro(re)claiming Loss"). Both of these studies take an embodied approach manifested in performative writing that asks the reader to *feel* the text. This approach is also taken in my performance ethnography of Chicana/o identities in North Carolina (Calafell "Disrupting the Dichotomy"), Willis' ethnography of "Latina/o Nights" in Ohio, and in my recent autobiographical performance of the immigration process after 9/11 (Calafell "Performing the Responsible Sponsor"). Similarly, Shane Moreman asks us to consider the contours of white/Latino identity through explorations of cultural hybridity ("*Chupa Mi Cacahuate*"; "Hybrid Performativity"). Both Bonim-Rodriguez and Cruz ("Mis Muertos") use performative writing to evoke personal and cultural memory.

Again my intent here is not to diminish the work of scholars such as José Esteban Muñoz, Diana Taylor, Coco Fusco, Guillermo Gomez-Pena, Alberto Sandoval-Sánchez, Nancy Saporta Sternbach, and Alicia Arrizon. Each of these scholars has been central in making conversations about performance, and especially Latina/o performance, happen. However, there remains much more discussion to be had within the realm of performance and everyday life, particularly within the realm of communication studies. There is a discussion that can move beyond staged or performance art as the object of study.

This overview makes it abundantly clear that more work needs to be done to bring Latina/o performance to the forefront. Part of this work necessitates a reinvigoration and reclamation of theories of identity. I elaborate upon my approach to the study of identity and how this approach informs my methodological and textual choices in this book and other projects.

Identity Matters, Performance Matters

Like others who study historically marginalized groups, I have often felt the backlash toward identity politics. While they have come under a great deal of attack, their work seen as divisive or "ideological fictions" (Alcoff and Mohanty), I, like Linda Martín Alcoff, Michael Hames-García, Satya Mohanty, and Paula Moya, am committed to reclaiming identity as a fruitful site of knowledge. Alcoff and Mohanty argue that "'experiences' are not unfathomable inner phenomena, but rather disguised explanations of social relations, and they can be evaluated as such" (5). They argue,

> Identities can be no less real for being social and historically situated, and for being
> relational, dynamic, and, at times, ideological entrapments.... [Identities] are not
> mere *descriptions* of who we are but, rather, *casual explanations* of our social locations
> in a world that is shaped by such locations, by the way they are distributed and
> hierarchically organized. The real debate is not over whether identities have political
> relevance, but how much and what kind. (6)

Inspired by these scholars' commitment to reinvesting in and reinvigorating theories of identity, I remain committed to thinking through and theorizing points of Latina/o performance. Rosaura Sánchez, in her essay "On a Critical Realist Theory of Identity," argues that though identity politics and can be manipulated by hegemonic forces, "a critical politics of identity can play a part in political organizing and in challenging hegemonic discourses, even if structural transformation is not the issue at hand in the short term" (33). Theories about Latina/o identities as they intersect with performance provide ample spaces for us to consider resistance and community. Thus, performance matters and identities matter, especially in the space of the everyday as people like my grandparents negotiate power-laden terrains.

As a critical scholar who sees performance studies as a site of intervention and radical research (Conquergood "Performance Studies"), I am excited about the possibilities of joining a Latina/o politics of identity with theories of performance to reflect upon issues such as affect, community building, diaspora, popular culture, and sexuality. Thus, though the subject of this book is Latina/o performance, it is not simply that. This is a text about identity, resistance, power, and performance. Like Conquergood, I believe that "performance studies struggles to open the space between analysis and action, and to pull the pin on the binary opposition between theory and practice. This embrace of different ways of knowing is radical because it cuts to the root of how knowledge is organized in the academy" ("Performance Studies" 146) Thus, in taking this approach, I operate from a varied understanding of text and method. In his own work, Frederick Corey argues that as a performance scholar he has tended to use textual analysis as guiding force; however, he defines text broadly to include "language, behavior, place, the body, and cultural landscape" ("On Possibility" 331). I follow Corey's lead in my approach to texts and method, heeding the words of Conquergood when he says, "For many people throughout the world, however, particularly subaltern groups, texts are often inaccessible, or threatening, charged with the regulatory powers of the state. More often than not, subordinate people experience texts and the bureaucracy of literacy as instruments of control and displacement" ("Performance Studies" 147).

Of this perspective, Barbara Christian writes,

> For people of color have always theorized—but in forms quite different from the Western form of abstract logic. And I am inclined to say that our theorizing ... is often in narrative forms, in the stories we create, in riddles and proverbs, in the play with language, since dynamic rather than fixed ideas seem more to our liking. How else have we managed to survive with such spiritedness the assault on our bodies, social institutions, countries, our very humanity? (336)

On the basis of both Conquergood's and Christian's insights, this collection illustrates my use of autobiographical performance, textual analysis of written documents, collection and analysis of oral narratives, and poetic transcription. My varied approach comes from an understanding that if we are going to reach the texts produced by historically marginalized communities, we must meet these texts on their own terms methodologically (Calafell and Delgado); we must understand that they may not take traditional or dominant forms (Christian; Conquergood "Performance Studies"; Ono and Sloop "The Critique"); and we as scholars must not be afraid to turn the glance inward.

In addition, though it is implied and understood as an aspect of a critical performance–centered perspective, I want to reaffirm my commitment to reflexivity. In considering reflexivity, I do not simply mean that as a researcher I consider how my multiple identities inform the way I come to see and understand the world; rather, I am trusting in what Cherríe Moraga and Gloria Anzaldúa term theories of the flesh and Patricia Hill Collins terms everyday intellectualizing. Furthermore, Moraga and Anzaldúa ask us to consider the theory of the flesh as a way to understand Other ways of knowing and theorizing. Defining the term in the groundbreaking anthology *This Bridge Called My Back*, Moraga and Anzaldúa write, "A theory in the flesh means one where the physical realities of our lives—our skin color, the land or concrete we grew up on, our sexual longings—all fuse to create a politic born out of necessity. Here we attempt to bridge the contradictions of our experience" (23). Anzaldúa elaborates on the theory of the flesh in her discussion of *conocimientos*, which, she argues,

> comes from opening all your senses, consciously inhabiting all your body and decoding its symptoms ... Attention is multileveled and includes your surroundings, bodily

> sensations and responses, intuitive takes, emotional reactions to other people and
> theirs to yours and, most important, the images your imagination creates—images
> connecting all tiers of information and their data. Breaking out of your mental and
> emotional prison and deepening the range of perception enables you to link inner
> reflection and vision—the mental, emotional, instinctive, imaginal, spiritual, and
> subtle bodily awareness—with social, political action and lived experience to gener-
> ate subversive knowledges. These conocimientios challenge official and conventional
> ways of looking at the world, ways set up by those benefiting from such constructions.
> (*This Bridge We Call Home* 542)

Theories of the flesh privilege subjectivity and embodied knowledges as sites
of fruitful theory building, giving women of color back the power to speak as
authorities about their own experiences, challenging, as Conquergood notes,
the intellectual's error of believing "that one can know without understanding and even more without feeling and being impassioned" ("Performance
Studies" 149).

Informed by these scholars, I draw upon my theories of the flesh as a
Chicana academic doing Chicana/o and Latina/o studies. Rather than performing what I believe to be a false "objective" stance, I fully embrace the ways
that my identities come to bear on not only how I see my texts but also how
I feel them. These theories of the flesh not only force me to be reflexive but
also make me passionate, and grant me a personal stake in the work that is part
of the commitment of a performance project—social justice.

The Contours of Latina/o Performance

Having briefly described my relationship to the field, my approach to the
study of identity and performance, and my methodological preferences, I want
to give an overview of the chapters of this book. I divide this book into two
sections. Part one, "Chicana/o Lived Experience: Reimagining Space and
History," includes chapter 2, "Transforming Landscapes through Performance:
'Yo Soy Chicana/o' in the New Latina/o South," a performance ethnography
using poetic transcription to examine the ways that Chicana/o identities are
performed in spaces that have little to no recognition of them. This work asks
us to consider the position of Chicana/os as both diasporic and non-diasporic
and to think about how Chicana/o as a term of identification may or may
not continue to shift or evolve given the increasing dispersal of Mexicans,
Mexican Americans, and Chicana/os across the country. Chapter 3, "Looking
For Marina/Looking For Myself: A Chicana Feminist Performance," uses

autobiographical performance to demonstrate the relationship between the story of Malintzin Tenépal, translator and lover of Hernan Cortés, and modern Chicanas' loss of voice and feelings of homelessness.

Part two, "The Stage We Call Our Lives: Performance and the Mass Consumption of Latina/o Identities," attempts to unpack the performance of Chicana/o and Latina/o identities that we see in popular culture. In chapter 4, "My Love/Hate Relationship with El Vez," I examine Chicano performance artist/Elvis Presley cultural translator El Vez, who has been widely celebrated in academic circles. I do attempt not so much to provide answers as to ask questions and consider the ways that the private personality of performer Robert Lopez works in conjunction with the larger-than-life image of El Vez to create complex and nuanced readings of Chicana/o identities. Chapter 5, "To Ricky with Love," takes a look at international singing sensation Ricky Martin and his performances of racial and sexual ambiguity during the 1999–2000 "Latin explosion" to understand the nuances of resistance and commodification. This chapter also ends with a letter to Martin recounting a performance piece I did in his honor. Chapter 6, "Reflecting on the (Im)possibilities of *Latinidad:* Affective Connections among Latina/os," raises some preliminary questions about pan-Latina/o identities through a discussion of the possible reappropriation of the term Latina/o in hip-hop and Reggaeton. I conclude in chapter 7 with some thoughts about the contributions of and the future of Latina/o performance. In each of these chapters I hope to demonstrate the varied landscape of Latina/o performance in terms of content and method.

PART I
CHICANA/O LIVED EXPERIENCE: REIMAGINING SPACE AND HISTORY

· 2 ·

TRANSFORMING LANDSCAPES THROUGH PERFORMANCE: "YO SOY CHICANA/O" IN THE NEW LATINA/O SOUTH

Mexican, Latina, Hispanic, Mexican American, Chicana … so many names, so many meanings. Each of these names has meant something different to me at different points in my life and I am sure will continue to do so. Other scholars, including Dolores Tanno, Susana Rinderle, and Jacqueline Martinez, have described various meanings and stages of coming to consciousness associated with labels for identity. Inspired by their stories, I reflect on my own, similar journey.

As a young child I first identified as Mexican because of the way my family spoke about our history and because Spanish and English were both spoken in my home. We were Mexican and that was all I knew. Though initially I did not know exactly where in Mexico we were from, I still identified very strongly with that label. However, on entering grade school I soon found that the majority of my peers in a largely Mexican American school distinguished themselves from the Mexican immigrants in the community by calling themselves Hispanic, while often using derogatory terms such as wetbacks to describe the others. High school came and so did the term Mexican American and with it all the assimilationist tendencies and the belief that if I really did work hard I could get what I wanted. The sad reality of this myth hit me in the face when, despite my good grades, I failed to earn a scholarship to the local university. The American Dream really was a myth that perpetuated false hope in anyone who dared to believe in it. My naivety was shattered with this experience.

Instead of moving a few hours away (this was unthinkable in my mind) to another college to which I had received a partial scholarship, I decided to venture to the local community college, which I could attend for free. After spending two years at the community college, I finally made it to the local university a little more jaded. Upon entering the campus and for the first time in my life being overwhelmed by the whiteness of the space, I sought refuge in classes that spoke to marginalized experiences—intercultural communication and Chicano studies. While some of my peers took these classes so they might look better on the job market because they had "experience with diversity," I took these courses as a survival strategy. It was through the study of the systematic nature of oppression that I began to identify with a Chicana standpoint.

A Chicana feminist perspective placed my experience as a woman of color at the center, allowing me to see myself not as a victim or someone with no history but as a strong woman with an illustrious but silenced history. Chicanas do have histories; we simply do not have access to them in dominant narratives. Allowing myself to delve into what had been positioned as taboo or Other helped me understand the various situations that operated around me socially and politically. Writers such as Ana Castillo, Gloria Anzaldúa, and, most important, Cherríe Moraga demonstrate how the legacy of colonialism has a direct effect on our everyday experiences as Chicanas. My reading of them marked my shift from assimilationist tendencies to a space that was more critical.

I continued down this path until I stepped foot in North Carolina and was forced, for the first time, really to identify myself as a Latina—a Latina in a space that negated Chicana identities. Latina was a term I had not previously used to describe myself because of its generality; it was a term that could refer to anyone of Mexican, Puerto Rican, Cuban, Dominican, or any other Latin American descent. Thus, in coming to North Carolina, a land whose population was unknown to me, I chose Latina because of the possibility of identification across ethnic groups. Rhetorical scholar Dolores Tanno, writing of her use of the term Latina, explains, "To use *Latina* is to communicate acceptance and belonging in a broad cultural community" (27). Thus, I chose this label strategically upon moving to North Carolina. Later, as I became more knowledgeable about Latina/o politics, not just Mexican American or Chicana/o politics, I came to believe in a politics of *latinidad* or pan-Latina/o identification.

Drawing on writings by Cuban Americans who have long theorized identities based on exile, performance, and memory, I argue that these frameworks are necessary for developing political identities for Latina/os in the South. As a multiracial people and culture, in most cases even more so than Chicana/os and Mexicans, and because of their diasporic situation, Cuban Americans have been forced to consider identity in ways that are more complex because of a more physically difficult relationship to the homeland. Often identities are established through a connection with a feeling—in this case, nostalgia and practice. The possibility in these practices and representation is what I hope to point to as a way to reconceptualize Chicana/o identities as well as pan-Latina/o politics. It is from this understanding of feeling or affect as a trope of identification that I read the narrative of Mario (whom I will introduce more fully later).

The Latina/o South

The South, historically a racially dichotomous society populated by African Americans and whites, has in recent times been influenced by an influx of Latina/o immigrants. For example, North Carolina, the site of study in this essay, is cited as the third fastest growing state in terms of Latina/o populations; five of the thirty U.S. counties that experienced the most rapid growth in these communities between 1990 and 1996 were in North Carolina (Latinos in North Carolina). According to census data, over the past ten years North Carolina's Latina/o population has increased 394 percent to 378,963 (Latinos in North Carolina). Census data indicate that Latina/os in North Carolina constitute 4.7 percent of the population (Fact Sheet). However, according to rough estimates based on birth data from the North Carolina Center for Health Statistics, Latina/os now constitute 5.4 percent of the total population in North Carolina, and their numbers have increased 442.25 percent over the past ten years to reach an estimated 416,147 (Latinos in North Carolina). As noted by New South Productions, these numbers account only for those Latina/os who live in North Carolina year round and not those who migrate back and forth from their respective homelands. Furthermore, North Carolina and its Latina/o population growth has been the subject of two recent documentaries, *Nuestra Communidad*, produced by New South Productions, and *The Divide*, produced by PBS. The South is a particularly attractive site for two main reasons, first because of the job opportunities and the possibilities for work in rural agricultural areas, and second because of growing social or familial networks. Industries in North Carolina offer many job opportunities; for example, in Mecklenburg County 75 percent of construction workers are Latina/o and more than 95 percent of agricultural workers are Mexican; in Blanton County more than 50 percent of the workers in meat processing are Latina/o (Latinos in North Carolina).

Moving to North Carolina from Arizona, a state with more than 25 percent of its population identifying as Hispanic in the 2000 census (Fact Sheet), firmly entrenched in a Chicana identity, I had no idea about the complexity of racial tensions in that place or that Latina/os even lived there. Questions regarding the possibility of Chicana/o as a political and cultural identification for the future suddenly became more and more apparent to me as I found myself in a world in which very few people knew what Chicana/o meant or identified in that way. What I found instead was a vibrant and growing community of Mexican, Central American, Latina/o, and Arab immigrants who were remaking the face of North Carolina and with it my assumptions about the face of the South. What would Chicana/o come to mean to those children born Mexican American in the South—the next generation? What would Aztlán, our physical and symbolic nation, mean to those who had never visited it or had no concept of it? Would Chicana/o as a term of identification survive once Mexican Americans had moved beyond the Southwest? Or, because of the multiple connections being made in contact zones such as North Carolina, would Chicana/o become something else, allowing a new political identification to emerge? These questions filled my mind during the three years I lived in North Carolina.

Against this backdrop, I examine some of these convergences and raise questions about the viability of Chicana/o identities in the new millennium. I do not intend to devalue the experiences of Latina/o immigrants in North Carolina, but I am concerned with the ways in which Latina/os born in the United States identify with, disidentify with, or create spaces within historically racially dichotomous sites. There is a new experience that has yet to be named. Born out of a specific historical context, *Chicanismo* may not be a viable option in these situations, especially if Mexican Americans or Chicana/os want to make political coalitions across Latina/o groups or generations in these spaces. *Chicanismo* has very little cultural currency or capital in the South because it is not a living or fluent discourse in that space at this time. Chicana/o identities do not carry the same meanings or weight in the South as they do in the Southwest, where Chicana/o is a living discourse because of the history of the Chicano movement and the shadow of the pervasive border. A Chicana/o generation has not matured yet, and this ideology may not ever mature in the South because of its historical and spatial contingency. As my friend and interviewee Mario, whose words I will share, stated, "I have met people that have grown up here [North Carolina] and they have no connection to Aztlán, no connection or no identification with the Chicano category." I share Mario's narrative in relationship to my own to bear witness to the experiences of displacement for Chicana/os in the South and to make a larger argument for a politics of affect and excess in these spaces that enable continual transcultural exchanges.

Rhetorical scholars Delgado, Hammerback and Jensen, and Flores have described the process by which the identification Chicana/o emerged. In the turbulent 1960s and 1970s, as a result of unfair labor, schooling, and political practices, the Chicano movement was born. Chicano, a formerly derogatory term for Mexicans in the United States, was reappropriated by activists as a strategy of empowerment. These discourses continued to flourish in the ensuing decades, as witnessed in the birth of the Chicana feminist movement. However, the majority of the work produced by the legacy of the movement, such as Anzaldúa's *Borderlands/La Frontera: The New Mestiza*, Moraga's *Loving in the War Years: Lo Que Nunca Paso Por Sus Labios* and *The Last Generation: Poetry and Prose*, and Gómez-Peña's *New World Border: Prophecies, Poems, Loqueras for the End of the Century*, understandably continued to focus on the Southwest, as it is viewed as both the real and the symbolic home of Chicana/os—Aztlán.

Commenting on Mexican and Chicana/o migrations, Pérez writes, "If diaspora, loosely defined, is a 'history of dispersal coupled with myths and memories of a homeland,' where 'alienation in the host country' often fosters a 'desire for eventual return' while a collective memory reconstructs the alienated group's history whether real or imagined, then Chicanos/as are appropriately diasporic" (78). Unlike other Latina/o groups in the United States, Chicana/os exist as both diasporic and non-diasporic citizens because they live in the Southwest, formerly Mexican land, and outside of it as well. In comparing the situation of Chicana/os, whose "homeland" may be here in the United States and right across the border, with Puerto Ricans and Cuban Americans, who have a long, documented history of diaspora and dispersal, it would be beneficial to examine the identity formations of these groups as a way to respond to changes in Chicana/o communities. A similar situation is described by Drzewiecka and Halualani, who write of Hawaiians as an indigenous group that can claim sovereign belonging to a land colonized by a dominant nation-state (351). This chapter seeks to expand and add complexity to this situation as well as to prior research on diaspora studies, which have traditionally focused on communities that have migrated from far away, by instead examining the regional dispersion of diaspora within the nation-state. Shome calls for rhetorical theories that are able to address the rhetorical situations and experiences of "disjunctured diasporic cultural identities" and asks how "cultural diasporas use rhetoric to negotiate through their different culturally disjunctured or pastiched states to enable some kind of shared meaning with people in their daily existence?" (601). This project is the first step in the development of Chicana/o diasporic experiences.

I begin with a description of my methodological approach, which is followed by the introduction of my interviewee, Mario, and a brief discussion of our relationship. I then provide a discussion of community and diaspora that serves to frame my analysis and conclude with a discussion of Mario's and my experiences as Chicana/os in North Carolina. I will argue that because of the lack of identification with a Chicana/o identity in North Carolina, Mario performed his identity with an "excessive zeal" (Torres-Saillant). Scholars such as Bhabha, Muñoz, and Lancaster have discussed the political possibilities of performances of excess as forms of resistance, and working from their assumptions I seek to examine the ways excess manifests when diaspora relocates to new and regional cultural contexts. As argued by these scholars, excess serves as a point of identification that enables community not only resistance. Mario's performance of excess allowed him to maintain a symbolic connection to the Southwest and the only other Chicano he knew: me. Interestingly, Mario's performance of Chicano identity was altered by his desire to connect with Mexican immigrants in North Carolina so he would have a sense of community, which resulted in an amalgamated version of identity that highlighted the importance of being Mexicano and Chicano, thus usurping tensions between these groups. In a sense, through these performances of excess Mario recrossed the border to gain a sense of community. Mario's narrative sheds light on the give-and-take transcultural exchanges that begin in these contact zones (Sandoval-Sánchez and Sternbach). Sandoval-Sánchez and Sternbach argue that transculturalism operates from a position of resistance and subversion and that cultures are fused, recycled, and reconverted in these processes. Mario's performances of excess also reinforced his position as foreign in the minds of the whites and African Americans he encountered. Conversely, this served to strengthen his connection with immigrant communities, as he could relate through the affect of the Other in a form heightened and different from the racism he had experienced before. I trace these movements through the following themes: *Yo Soy Chicano y Mexicano*, examines the ways Mario acknowledges and bridges the tensions between Chicana/os and Mexicana/os to gain a larger identification and community; *A Case of Diasporic Intimacy: "You Are My Chicano Space,"* examines the ways in which Mario holds on to the rhetoric of *Chicanismo* and the Southwest while maintaining his connection to Mexican immigrant communities; and *Forever Foreign: A Stereotypical Mexican,* demonstrates the ways in which Mario's interactions with other communities, African American and white, strengthened his connection to Mexican communities through an affect of foreignness. I conclude with a section that describes Mario's return to Aztlán.

Methodological Approach

Conquergood writes, "Dialogical performance is a way of having intimate conversation with other people and cultures. Instead of speaking about them, one speaks to and with them. The sensuous immediacy and empathic leap demanded by performance is an occasion for orchestrating two voices, for bringing together two sensibilities" ("Performing As a Moral Act" 10). A dialogic approach to ethnography attempts to account for reflexivity and to negotiate the politics of voice through its denial of authority to any one voice. Conquergood elaborates this point by stating that within ethnographic practice the general move is to "recuperate the saying from the said," which mobilizes and gives action and agency to the words of the people (31). Thus, words remain alive as they are embodied, unfixed with meaning or authority. Madison asks that we understand "the embodied self ... a voice wedded to experience" ("Performance, Personal Narrative" 278). A performance ethnography paradigm or dialogical performance "is a vivid reminder that each voice has its own integrity" (Conquergood "Performing as a Moral Act" 10). Furthermore, Madison reminds us that as critical ethnographers, "we do not hide our selfhood and subjectivity, transparency is not an issue, nor do we make ourselves the primary subject of our own study. Instead, we are critical and self-reflexive of *how* we think about our positionality and the implications of our thoughts and judgments" ("The Dialogic Performative" 322). However, the call for reflexivity in performance ethnography is heightened as it is made through the conjunction of the mind and body that "requires variously sensuous retellings and ongoing re-creations, in work and body" (Pollock "Marking New Directions" 325). This reflexive participatory knowledge privileges not only less traditionally accepted practices of theorizing but also Other ways of knowing by challenging the mind/body split. It also gives authority to Other kinds of texts or what are termed cultural performances, which have often been overlooked because of a bias toward textuality. Thus, participatory epistemology allows the ethnographer access not only to other ways of knowing him or herself but also to various types of texts, both oral and written, such as cultural performances. The value of a participatory perspective is its attention to the practices of the everyday and the affect associated with those practices.

Informed by a performance ethnography paradigm I use poetic transcription for the interviews I include in this project. This poetic transcription is modeled after the work of performance scholar D. Soyini Madison in her essays "That Was My Occupation: Oral Narrative, Performance, and Black Feminist Thought" and "Story, History, and Performance: Interpreting Oral History through Black Performance Traditions." Describing her choice to use poetic transcription, Madison writes,

> Poetic text is consistent with the black tradition of acknowledging that words are alive with sounds that condition their meanings. By placing words on a page in a way that resembles the rhythm of the human voice and the speaker as a social-historical being who colors each word based on that existential fact, the text comes closer to capturing the depth inherent in the indigenous performance of black speech. ("That Was My Occupation" 323)

Madison's use of poetic transcription privileges orality and specific speech patterns. This transcription embodies through words the importance of the gestures and meanings that are performed and communicated in interviews. This vernacular discourse does not divorce language or words from their embodied nature. Madison argues, "In poetic form, words are not in isolation from movement, sound, and sensory body that give them substance. Words are not placed on a page in blocks of prose divorcing them from the actions and meanings of their speaker" ("Story, History, and Performance" 46). The performance aspect of this transcription is central because it grants ownership of the words to the speaker rather than a researcher who has taken them and put them on the page as he or she pleases. These transcriptions materialize experience in their performance ("That Was My Occupation" 344). My desire in using this method is to highlight certain meaning and rhythms in language and the choice of words while privileging the importance of orality in historically marginalized cultures.

Working from a perspective informed by the traditions I have described, I spent three years in North Carolina examining the convergences of Latina/os in the state. However, it was during my first year that I conducted interviews primarily with Mario, whose words will be shared here. Over the next two years I conducted interviews and conversations with other Latina/os who identified as Chicana/o, Puerto Rican, Hispanic, and Mexican, about their experience in North Carolina. These interviews and conversations arose from informal or snowball methods. In assuming a participatory perspective, I also partook in rituals both public and private (with Mario as well as in the larger community), such as Spanish mass at the local Catholic Church, Latina/o nights at local clubs, and community festivals. I also kept a journal about the nature of home for Chicana/os in the South. In focusing on Mario's narrative, as well as my own experience, I assumed a performance ethnography approach that allowed my insights or reflexivity as a Chicana in the South to help me make sense of what I was observing and participating in. While I conducted a series of interviews with Mario, from which many of these narratives are drawn, the majority of what I considered to be my deepest insight was gained through our everyday conversations and the performative process of being involved in day-to-day activities with each other. As Mario and I were both situated in the privileged site of the university, both doctoral students, we were constantly reflecting on our sense of alienation, attempting to find ways to work through it, and even to explain what we saw all around us. As I operated from a performance perspective, much of the knowledge I gained in my three years was embodied. Thus, in sharing Mario's words and describing certain scenarios, I hope to evoke the feelings or affects through which I came to understand what was happening to us.

"The embrace of hybridity, liminality, the celebration of one's exoticism at home, substitutes for the production of actual analysis. ..." (di Leonardo 312). She could finish the sentence. She knew the criticisms offered by di Leonardo. They were the same charges that always get leveled at this type of work. Does the term "the new Narcissae" ring a bell? Oh you know, irreverent, self-absorbed, sentimental. These are all the words Carolyn Ellis and Art Bochner answer to for their writing. Now a year later, she faces the charges again, only this time they come from within and every once and a while certain mentor who questions the politics of narcissism. Ethnography is a spiritual experience, the body becomes our instrument, our way of knowing; thus, we must explore our subjectivities so we can honor those who share their stories with us. Like Ellis, she wants to enter and document the moment-to-moment, concrete

details of life (Ellis and Bochner 737), but at the same time, like Dwight Conquergood, she wants to engage another voice in intimate conversation ("Performing As a Moral Act").

Ruth Behar writes that anthropology that doesn't break your heart is just not worth doing. Well, her heart is broken. In class she staunchly defended Sarah Lawrence-Lightfoot's book; now it has hit her—the criticisms—as she looks at her computer screen. Has she romanticized him? Has she idealized him and made him all she wanted him to be? It all started very simply. It was a friendship. Initially, they couldn't get enough of each other. Every weekend, every other day. And then, sometimes it was every other weekend. The friendship was intense already, but what would happen when they began to theorize their experiences? When they moved their friendship into a different context? She would spend time with him, interview him, and find ways to consider how the experiences of being out of Aztlán shaped identity. She wanted to have a conversation of experiences—hers and his. She wanted to know how one might perform or practice an identity that has yet to be really articulated in this space, but it became more than that. It seems it always does. Yes, Anzaldúa, de Certeau, Moraga, and Muñoz all come to mind when she considers ways to think about theorizing the project, but so do Behar and Lawrence-Lightfoot. The questions are not so much about identity any more as they are about vulnerability, respect, and space.

Having described my ethnographic approach and situated this project within my larger study, I will briefly describe the landscape of our world in North Carolina. There I lived in what is commonly known as the Research Triangle, or the Raleigh-Durham Area. Attending graduate school in Chapel Hill, I lived in Carrboro—a suburb. One needed only literally to cross the railroad tracks to enter the more ethnically diverse community of Carrboro. According to data from the U.S. Census and the City of Carrboro,

> Carrboro has the highest Hispanic/Latino population in Orange county with 2,062. This was a 936 percent increase from 1990 when the Hispanic/Latino population was 199. This group accounts for 12.3 percent of the population. Specifically, those with a Mexican origin have increased from 64 in 1990 to 1,530 in 2000. That is a 2,291 percent increase. This sub-group accounts for 9.1 percent of the population in Carrboro. ("Ethnic and Community Development")

The growth of the Latina/o community in Carrboro has not gone unnoticed; as recently as May 2003 the town produced an assessment and documents discussing ways to better meet the needs of the Latino community. Carrboro, with its burgeoning Latina/o community, was the closest thing I could find to home in North Carolina.

Within the confines of Carrboro you could easily locate several *tiendas Mexicanas* and Mexican restaurants that catered to the growing communities. It was also within Carrboro that the annual Fiesta de los Pueblos was held.

Every morning as I rode the bus to school, I would look out the window at the corner store and see as many as twenty Mexican men waiting for work for the day. These scenes and the feelings they evoked were the closest thing I had to south Phoenix. While some of my more affluent students questioned why I would live in such an area, I affirmed that it was exactly what I needed to keep myself alive spiritually and culturally. Carrboro, with its sense of community, as well as the local Catholic church, is where my interviewee Mario and I spent the majority of our time.

In addition to Carrboro, Mario and I spent much of our time at the university, a few minutes away. The disparity between the growing numbers of Latina/os in the Carrboro and Chapel Hill areas should be noted; according to the Office of Institutional Research of the university, only 1.6 percent of students in the fall of 2000 were Hispanic ("Distribution of Students"). I share these numbers to illustrate the lack of community present for Mario and myself during the first semester we met and to give testimony to the disparity between what was happening in the community and what was happening in the university.

The Forming of Other Communities

This journey began some time ago; perhaps it began that first moment when I drove into the utter darkness of the North Carolina woods wondering what I had gotten myself into and asking myself whether it would be too late to go back. Maybe the journey began when I met him, another Chicano exile in North Carolina. Regardless of the actual point of origin, I can characterize this journey by emotions: loss, mourning, loneliness, and solitude. Play a song, say a word, tell a story, and I am taken back to that same feeling of not being quite right, of being displaced. I share these details because they are incredibly relevant in telling the story of how I came to think about Mexican American identities in terms of *performance* rather than land or racial essences. In North Carolina Mario and I were performing to create feelings or affects of community. Moving to North Carolina (whose population's only conception of Latina/o was largely built upon the influx of a Mexican immigrant community, Jennifer Lopez, and Ricky Martin) in August 2000, I never realized the impact a racially dichotomous society would have on my self-definition. My identity was so entrenched in Chicana rhetoric and the Southwest that I was not prepared for what I would encounter. My desire for home and for certainty was marked clearly in my journal entry of the first trip back to Arizona in fall break of 2000:

> Away for two months of spiritual emptiness, in her journal *la guera*, newly transplanted in North Carolina writes, "I am home. I am back in Aztlán." I got teary eyed when I began to recognize the buildings as the plane slowly descended. I was looking at myself, the mountains and the desert, they are and were me. I am Pat Mora's desert woman and I have never had such clarity.... I remember when I was driving with Felicia I wanted to write a song like *Precosia*—now I know why Marc Anthony sings it with such passion—he loves the land, Puerto Rico is a part of him and he cannot conceive of himself without it. Leaving this land I leave a part of my soul behind, but now I take it back. I reclaim it. She now knows that Aztlán can be a physical place and a state of mind. Relishing the experience of being in the homeland, she met with friends to share her experience of *that other place*. They looked at the pictures and said, "You have never looked happier. You must be happy all you talk about is that place." *If only they knew as Chicana feminist poet Pat Mora knew that "even in inhospitable places, cactus bears fruit."* (Nepantla 294)

Pina writes that the story of Aztlán "relates the sacred history of the Aztecs' peregrination from a northern homeland Aztlán, to the founding of the empire of Tenochtitlan" (38). It was not only this sacred history that I longed for with each return to Arizona, but also the familiarity the Southwest offered. While Chicana/o experiences in the Southwest are greatly informed by the history of Aztlán, they can also be characterized by the pervasive border (as written about by Anzaldúa) that serves as a larger metaphor for biculturalism or the recognition and performance of identities that are informed by both Mexico and the United States, as well as a unique border culture. Chicana/o experiences in the Southwest are characterized by their urbanity/suburbanity, whereas in the South migration and ruralness are the common tropes. In addition, there are the architectural differences, services, community/population, and living history that all speak the language of *Chicanismo*. This familiarity, the presence of the border that somehow signaled my rightful place in the space that was and is my homeland simultaneously, despite its changing meanings, characterized what I missed most about the Southwest. Of the Latina/os living in the United States, 50 percent live in the southwestern states California and Texas, with Arizona being one of the states with a population of more than a million (Fact for Features). The sheer numbers, the history, and the frequent use of Spanish create an environment where one never has to really think about his or her identity as it is given and supported in the everyday.[1] It is similar to a situation described by Herrera in her book *Remembering Cuba: Legacy of a Diaspora*, in which she interviews Cuban American exiles about their experiences growing up displaced. Herrera writes, "Their exile consciousness, therefore, can be attributed both to the physical proximity of Miami to the Island, and to the fact that they were socialized in a socioeconomic environment that reinforces a particularly strong sense of Cuban cultural identity. As a result, quite a few pointed out that when they are in Miami, they never have to think about their identities" (xxiii). Anzaldúa, commenting on this legacy and the history of the land writes, "This land was Mexican once, was Indian always and is. And will be again" (*Borderlands* 3). As for hundreds of other Chicana/os in the Southwest, the history of the land and the border defined my experience, my space in the middle, my ambiguity and empowerment. Without its constant presence to "authenticate" and inform my identity, I was lost.

Unable to return home, looking for some point of identification, for some kindred soul, I quickly made friends with the few other Latina/o graduate students in the area. One of these relationships in particular led me to ask questions regarding the necessity of performance as a means to create and maintain identities and communities for diasporic citizens. As diasporic citizens, through rituals such as the creation of altars, attending Catholic mass in Spanish, and telling stories (these rituals that I had not participated in while living in the Southwest suddenly became of extreme importance to my everyday experience), Mario and I found that the spaces between two bodies could be the space exiles long for. These desired spaces provided the self-knowledge, familiarity, and comfort necessary for the survival of exiles. Through the use of familiar religious symbols and practices in spaces that were explicitly Latina/o, such as Spanish mass, we found familiarity that took us back home. These spaces and this familiarity helped recuperate what we had lost in being away from home. What I came to realize over the course of the three years of this project was that home was no longer a physical space but the feeling or affect created through the community of loss Mario and I formed, as well as the feelings of Otherness shared with other Latina/os. What we continually desired under the guise of home were feelings of familiarity and community we had taken for granted in the Southwest.

Writing of the experiences of exiles in diasporic situations, Sara Ahmed, author of *Strange Encounters: Embodied Others in Post-Coloniality*, notes, "The forming of a new community provides a sense of fixity through the language of heritage—a sense of inheriting a collective past by sharing the lack of a home rather than sharing a home" (85). Furthermore, through the telling of stories and the production of a "we," memory becomes a space for reflection

(91). Through the performance of telling, the production of a "we," memory is critiqued, enabling rhetorics of possibility and actualization. Langellier marks this as the possibility of performance in that the illusion of the self as stable and persistent comes into being—the voice that needs a body is given one. These theories serve as the context for understanding our need for community in North Carolina, though initially we thought none existed. In our private performances of memory and the mythology of the Southwest, Mario and I were activating community with each word and creating spaces for Chicana/o identifications in a land with no conception of them. The practicality of our nostalgia was that it produced community and familiarity within the unfamiliar.

These spaces kept us alive. These spaces sustained us. Pérez, writing of the importance of the mythology of Aztlán for diasporic subjects, notes,

> The diasporic subject reminds us that Aztlán, the mythic homeland shifts and moves beneath and around us. The mythic homeland is longed for, constructed, and rewritten through collective memories. Time is traversed, and a mythic past entwines with a future where a decolonized imaginary has possibilities. (78)

The forging of our community through nostalgic performance can be likened to Robert Richmond Ellis' discussion of the *ambiente* as "a common space arising through a reciprocity of praxis" (3) that "can be experienced only collectively even if this collectivity is initially private. Reading the ambiente is hence less an act of 'outing' than of 'joining' in a process of generating a social space" (4). Rodriguez argues that the *ambiente* speaks to a larger community and a sense of belonging (*Queer Latinidad* 26). Thus, the *ambiente* can mirror de Certeau's description of the power of stories to transform space and place for diasporic exiles. Our desire for the homeland concretized our identifications and community with one another and larger Latina/o communities.

However, these practices were not just about the community of loss forged in the practice of ritual and story but also the feelings associated with that loss. Writing of the power of performance, memory, and affect, José Esteban Muñoz states that for queers of color, memory is not static; it functions as space where the self is continually refashioned and politics can be imagined ("Memory Performance" 100). He argues, "While memory is not static for anyone, it is always 'in the making' for the minoritarian subject, who cannot perform normative citizenship and thus has no access to the standardized narratives of national cultural memory" (100). Muñoz asserts that standard models of citizenship in the United States are based on a national affect centered on white middle-class subjectivity ("Feeling Brown" 69). He argues that the "often off" or anti-normative affect of Latina/os is based upon an idea of excess or disidentification, while I argue that this affect is based on a queer temporality or the sense of "not being on time" or being written outside of the master narrative. While Muñoz favors the performative possibilities of difference as embodied in and through excess, I take this a step further to look toward the performative possibilities of memory to re-center difference ("Memory Performance"). Calling for a view of identity as affective difference, Muñoz gestures toward the study of lived experience. Articulating *latinidad*, Muñoz is concerned with collective affective performance, which demonstrates that Latina/o performativity "is not about race, region, gender, language, or any other easily identifiable demarcation of 'difference.' Thinking of latinidad as anti-normative affect engenders a model of group identity that is not exclusionary, yet still coherent" ("Memory Performance" 100). In turning to *latinidad* Muñoz moves toward a performative identity politics not based on more "typical" spaces of identification in order to work through possible problems of essentialism. Difference and its resulting feelings become the axis of identification rather than what Muñoz terms easily identifiable demarcations of difference such as race ("Memory Performance"). Muñoz notes that this affect or space of possibility is a mode of belonging made possible through a mode of identification or disidentification. This anti-normative affect, compounded by our feelings of estrangement as a result of being in a new space, created a feeling that enabled the forging of our community and larger identifications. This feeling enabled by our performances and shared sense of loss mirrors what Boym terms diasporic intimacy.

Looking back now at the experience of our intense friendship forged around a shared sense of loss and mourning for home, I see that each of us was in search of some sort of authenticity. My use of the term authenticity is self-reflexive and aware of its social constructedness and its use as mythology. Authenticity came to represent the desired difference that remained as a space of lack. Thus, the search or desire for authenticity became a performative process that is in itself a marker of difference. Only later, when I left North Carolina, did I realize the search was futile and it was desire or the awareness of the futility that drove me. This sentiment is reminiscent of Moraga's words, which allude to the desire for "authenticity" many a Chicana/o experiences: "I am always hungry and shamed by my hunger for the Mexican woman I miss in myself" (*The Last Generation* 121). I had felt that way once before about another friend, a woman born in Mexico now living in the United States—her desire for my whiteness and my desire for her "Mexicanness." What we desired were bodies that made us feel at home, bodies that understood our cultures. Coming to North Carolina there were essentially no Chicana/o spaces because those identities really had yet to be realized in this part of the country, and they may never be realized. Thus, I was immediately drawn to the only other person I met who identified as Chicano. I met him through an acquaintance, and from that point on we became inseparable. Perhaps it was because he looked so familiar. Perhaps it was because he seemed like everything I needed at that time. Whatever the case, I felt he was a godsend. He became one my best friends, my confidante, and my brother. As a Chicano from Los Angeles, his vivid descriptions of his life in North Carolina resonated so much with my own experiences. Interestingly, I have always had a sinking suspicion that if Mario and I had met in the Southwest we would not have been friends—perhaps acquaintances at the most. He was more of a Chicano nationalist than I was, and I fear he would not have been able to get past my whiteness. But because we were in North Carolina we had no other choice.

Explicitly identifying himself as Chicano, Mario defined the term as very political: "It means the reaffirmation, it means resistance to the dominant discourse. It means in a way at least partially self naming and self-definition and self autonomy." Comparing his experience of being Chicano in the Southwest with his experience in North Carolina, Mario stated, "It's like night and day I think." Whereas in California Mario did not feel the need to explain what he means when he calls himself Chicano, "in North Carolina it's isolating. It's umm, I mean people don't even know what Hispanic is. I think people know very little and make minimal effort to know anything about the differences within Latino cultures." While Mario noted that the majority of people in North Carolina lack familiarity with Latina/o cultures, he was aware of the large population of Latina/o immigrants and sought to make connections with that group:

> I think *for me* it's easier than for others
> because my parents were the immigrant generation.
> And I have a full command of different forms of Spanish.
> So … I can … I can relate
> and
> draw bridges

between those people and myself,
but it is it is still hard. Umm
I went through a
whole year here
before I even met
other
immigrants and Latinos
because my context is the context of the university.
My issues are very different from the
real life experiences
and labor
that that you know
first generation immigrants go through.
But like I said
because of my parents being an immigrant generation
I found it to be easier for me because …
I shared different … like I said forms of speech,
you know like rural Mexican speech,
umm and other forms of
like cultural …
cultural capital
that pertain to first generation immigrants.

Mario's identification with immigrant populations, a result of his status as first-generation Mexican American, is significant; it is not an experience to which all Chicana/os and Mexican Americans are privy. Very pervasive in Mexican American communities is the desire to distance oneself from Mexican communities as a way to establish an American or assimilationist identity in the eyes of the dominant culture. Many Mexican Americans and Chicana/os have lost their ties to Mexico. This situation is ambivalent as there is a desire to distance oneself from the Other while simultaneously having a tangible tie to that same Other. However, Mario's experience is more complex than this as it speaks not only to a sense of biculturalism, the ability to speak within the dominant culture and Chicana/o cultures, but also to the ability to speak with and to immigrant experiences. His view, much like that of performance artist Guillermo Gómez-Peña, disrupts static lines that divide Chicana/o and Mexican communities. Within Chicana/o communities the tension is not along the lines of assimilation, but quite the opposite. Chicana/os are often viewed as *pochos*, inauthentic, or American by Mexicans, who might ridicule their desire to return to a precolonial past.

A Case of Diasporic Intimacy: "You Are My Chicano Space"

Meeting Mario, I was reminded of the novel *The Greatest Performance*. It is a story of friendship, memory performance, and survival among queer Cuban American exiles. One section in particular characterized the nature of our relationship: "Look at this picture. See that cute guy there, in the back, behind Maritza? He's the one. My buddy. In my childhood story you have become that kid, Marito. Or rather, he has become you. And I can no longer remember his real name" (16). In this new place he literally and figuratively became my Mario. He became very special to me, helping me work through the isolation and loneliness I was going through in North Carolina. Much like the characters in *The Greatest Performance*, through our imagined pasts, renegotiated memories, and spaces of identification we created a sense of community in the space. Together we created Aztlán . . . even in North Carolina:

> Because my parents are the immigrant generation,
> I have all these ...
> different selves.
> There are times when I like to hang out with people who are
> Mexican and speak Spanish.
> But I always . . .
> when I was here by myself,
> I always felt like there was a part of me that
> was *ignored*.
> You know, and a part of me . . . that
> I couldn't talk to anyone else about
> and
> when I met your friend
> I was so happy.
> I was like, "Oh my God!"
> And we talked and talked and this and that and
> even though she wasn't Chicana
> I felt like we understood each other in a way
> And then when she told me she had a friend in the same program
> who was Chicana
> I was like waiting for you to call and
> then when you finally *DID*
> and
> we went out to dinner,
> we were talking about Cherrie Moraga ... and other people we knew of

. . . the Chicano scholar canon I guess.
And we didn't have to be explaining,
"you know
Chicano means this ____"
I mean it was just awesome.
You know.
It was cool.
It really transformed my space.
And you know, all this shit happened and all that
but at the same time
I negotiate my spaces
. . . like you are my Chicano space.
This right now is my Chicano space.
Sometimes I still go to my Mexican space,
I found like right now I am in a very balanced situation
and
you continue to form part of that balance with
those other people
who have impacted my life here.

De Certeau writes of the ways in which space is a practiced place. He writes that stories "carry out a labor that constantly transforms places into spaces or spaces into places" (118). Mario's description of how the relationship transformed the space of North Carolina echoes Ahmed's assertion that for exiles, often the forming of new communities is built upon a shared sense of loss rather than an actual home itself. Though Mario and I romanticized the Southwest as our shared home, many of the rituals were bound up in the sense of loss or desire rather than the actual home itself, as our experiences as a first-generation man from California and a third-generation woman from Arizona, respectively, were vastly different.

Boym characterizes desire as a property of diasporic intimacy: "furtive pleasure of exile." This intimacy is marked by uprootedness and defamiliarization and can be approached only through "indirection and intimation, through stories and secrets." It is a precarious affection aware of its transience that thrives on unpredictable chance encounters hoping for understanding. It "reflects collective frameworks of memory that encapsulate even the most personal of dreams" (227–228). Our diasporic intimacy was a continual revisiting of pain. Pain worked through or purged in constant renegotiations or rituals. Thus, through the stories we shared, we created an *ambiente* that enabled a space of survival, which is what Pérez notes as being important in the mythology of Aztlán. The thing longed for, the space of loss, is manifested as the geography changes:

> It's interesting how we transform
> the spaces we are in,
> not just in our homes,
> but there have been times when I have been with friends here
> who are Mexican and
> the parents are there and
> the kids are there with their families
> and
> everybody's eating, we're eating Mexican food and
> like there's Spanish music on the radio
> and
> it doesn't seem like it's here you know.
> It's like it could be … it could be …
> New York,
> it could be …
> Texas,
> it could be …
> East LA
> and it's THOSE moments
> I feel no matter how tough things are,
> no matter how oppressive conditions are
> we always survive
> and
> we live on
> and
> we continue to live on.
> Well we live on because we live on.
> And you know what we are,
> we bring with us

Mario's statement that "we live on because we live on" reflects the conjunction of theory and practice in the lives of many persons of color. This conjunction illustrates what Moraga and Anzaldúa term theories of the flesh. These indigenous ways of coping, surviving, and resisting have been acquired through years of experience with oppression. Thus, Mario's statement echoes the importance of experience and the ways that bodies respond or make do in potentially oppressive situations. Anzaldúa writes of the *mestiza's* tolerance for ambiguity as she inhabits borderlands that are "vague and undetermined" places "created by the residue of an unnatural boundary." The borderland is in "a constant state of transition" (*Borderlands* 3). Living in the borderlands, acknowledging multiple subjectivities, the new *mestiza* need not worry about the loss of home because, as Anzaldúa writes, "I am a turtle, wherever I go I carry 'home' on my back" (21). Thus, as noted by Behar, our bodies become homelands, places "where knowledge, memory, and pain" are stored (139). Mario's statement demonstrates the tolerance of ambiguity privileging the body as a site of knowledge.

Perhaps expanding the idea of a tolerance for ambiguity, Chela Sandoval writes about the ways that people of color have developed what she terms a differential consciousness. Sandoval explains,

> I think of this activity of consciousness as the "differential," insofar as it enables movement "between and among" ideological positioning considered as variables, in order to disclose the distinctions among them. … The differential represents the variant; its presence emerges out of correlations, intensities, junctures, crises. Yet the differential depends on a form of agency that is self-consciously mobilized in order to enlist and secure influence; the differential is thus performative. (58)

The differential can be likened to the possibility of Otherness and the excess enabled by the affect of the Other. This excess allows mobility because it is tied to no one identity in particular. Thus, this differential excess is a strategic performative logic that enables resistance, allowing agency while simultaneously acting as a strategy of survival for those who employ it. This differential consciousness operates in ways similar to José Esteban Muñoz's model of disidentification, which assumes that people create spaces of meaning and identification within potentially oppressive texts in ways that are resistive (*Disidentifications*). Informed by the situation of diasporic intimacy as well as various theories of consciousness, I read the following narratives from Mario to locate the ways that he negotiates his spaces and identities.

Forever Foreign: The Stereotypical Mexican

In several of our discussions, Mario described an incident that was significant for him because in his opinion it defined his experiences in North Carolina and the ways that he was viewed racially and ethnically. He had a disagreement of opinion in a classroom during which it was perceived that he took the side of a white female over an African American male. After being questioned about his perceived disloyalty, Mario became introspective, questioning his actions in the incident. Though the incident is highly significant, I choose to focus on what I term the working through of the trauma of the incident. After describing the incident in the classroom, Mario then shared how he worked through what had happened:

> So then when it exploded
> like that I didn't know
> *what* to do,
> me and the white girl just thought of killing ourselves,
>   (*Laughing.*)
> driving off a cliff …
> and *really really* questioning ourselves
> if we had done something wrong
> you know and how.
> If we had really fucked up
> maybe.
> You know?
> And like trying to think of it from all different angles.
> So what we did was
> we got in the truck
> and we drove
> and the only thing I could think of that reminded
> me of home
> that brought me peace
> was the beach.
> So instead of driving half an hour
> like I do at home
> I drove *two hours*
> to go to the beach.
> And when we got there I didn't even know where I was
> I just followed until I got to the ocean.
> And I had with me seven pennies,
> and I had with me a candle
> that I went to pick up at my house, and some incense.
> I figured since
> he was a black man
> I went to go make peace
> with the African goddess of the sea.
> Yemoja.
> And I went
> and I made my offering.
> I dug a hole in the sand and I lit the candle.
> And it was lit,

You know I offered the pennies.
I burned the incense,
and
I waited for the tide to rise.
I don't know how long I waited
but the tide rose
and she came out
and she collected her dues.
And … I knew
I knew then that things were going to be okay.
I mean …
it wasn't going to be *perfect,*
but things were going to be *okay.*
And that was just like
such a …
key moment.
You know?
I didn't sleep that night. . . .
I drove back
and we got back at like six or seven in the morning.
And we had class that night.
But it was so intense.
And like I sought refuge in like my
spirituality
the way that I knew I could make peace with
myself.

Atonement. Forgiveness. Mario shared the fact that these practices were things he had done at home in Los Angeles to help calm himself for many years. He assured me that he was not a *brujo,* but he found these rituals comforting. Mario's desire to reconnect with home by way of North Carolina took him to the waters, the symbolic cleansing force and symbol of renewal. The ocean as an artifact of the Southwest works through the trauma associated with being outside of the Southwest, outside of "home," in an unfamiliar and unwelcoming space. Those spiritual practices handed down from Mexico to the Southwest are re-performed in this hostile environment as a way of making do and creating a sense of place. Schechner argues that rituals are a way to remember (45). Rituals are memories in action that help people deal with "difficult transitions, ambivalent relationships, hierarchies, and desires that trouble, exceed, or violate the norms of daily life" (45). Mario's ritual, as well as his description of taking "refuge in the church" as a space that allowed him to be "around so many other brown bodies" because "you know makes that space kind of sacred," demonstrates his commitment to making North Carolina a habitable Chicano space by finding spaces of community and possibility.

These rituals exemplify the kind of liminality in which "persons are stripped of their former identities and assigned places in the social world; they enter a time place where they are not-this-not-that, neither here nor there, in the midst of a journey from one social self to another" (Fanon 57–58). In *The Wretched of the Earth*, Fanon argues that within the decolonial process colonized persons will have the tendency to return to a national culture based upon a precolonial past as a means to sustain their identities in the present. In a similar manner, when speaking about this ritual, Mario marked it as something that connected him not only to the Southwest and to Chicana/o identity but also to a larger indigenous past that privileged the spiritual power of nature and ritual. Thus, in performing this ritual, Mario was making a connection with an indigenous Mexican past as well as what he would later elaborate as a history of mysticism or *curanderismo*—a belief in the healing power of natural elements.

Similarly, Love and Kohn write about tourists' uses of souvenirs as a means to hold onto the Other and as a point of nostalgia. Though they raise provocative questions, their insights can be furthered by questioning the ways Others use souvenirs aimed at the tourist to authenticate themselves:

> I read this book on imperialism and historical legacy in education
> by this guy John Lowinski
> and I would go home every night
> and I would look at my apartment....
> the things I have in there.
> I have serapes,
> I have La Virgen de Guadalupe,
> I have candles everywhere.
> You know and I mean
> some of those things are things that
> my mom would not hang up.
> So I started thinking you know,
> I wonder if we learn to exoticize ourselves
> or if we learn to accentuate those aspects of our history that
> we were traditionally taught to dislike.
> And then, at first I was like,
> "Am I being part of the imperialistic project and

exoticizing myself?
Am I buying into the travel channel,
you know, let me hang my prizes on the wall?"
Then I thought no, no
I like these things.
They're mine. You know a lot of them I made myself. . . .
And I have all of these things that somehow little by little remind me of
home.

Mario's words resonated with my experience; I vividly remember traveling to a Mexican border town before moving to North Carolina so I could buy items that suddenly seemed so essential to my move and my identity. Mario's embracement of all things he believed to exemplify Mexican identity or *Chicanismo* forced him reflexively to question his motivations and his purposeful uses of excess.

Mario's self-conscious performance of identity mirrors Battaglia's discussion of practical nostalgia. Practical nostalgia describes how planting served as a way to allow exiles to remain connected to home. This practicality tempered the dangers of narcissism and pity, constantly forcing reflexivity. Through its performance or practicality, memory is freed of its abstractness, in turn mitigating the dangers of nostalgia such as narcissism and impracticality. These theories help illuminate the necessity of Mario's performances of excess *Chicanismo*.

In a similar manner, Sunday mass at the local Catholic church or special days such as the ceremony honoring La Virgen de Guadalupe were the only days that Mario "felt like strong emotion inside of me, really I was gonna cry. You know I just … it was beautiful. It was beautiful. You know and to me I just love, sometimes I wish the mass would have lasted four or five hours. 'Cause that was the only moment that I felt happy or content or safe in that space." Mario's description of the sense of community enabled by the presence of "brown bodies" regardless of origin, generation, or citizenship mirrors how Aparicio defines *latinidad* "as a concept that allows us to explore moments of convergences and divergences in the formation of Latino/a (post)colonial subjectivities and in hybrid cultural expressions among various Latino national groups" (93). *Latinidad* manifested in cultural texts "evokes in its audience, and perhaps to its interpreter, an analogous structure of feeling having to with the pain of exile and of geocultural displacements" (93). An example might be singer Marc Anthony's song *Preciosa*, an ode to Puerto Rico and Puerto Rican nationalism, which can also be embraced by other Latina/os as a way to express a sense of feeling connected to homelands or displacement (93). Thus, Mario's excesses were not simply a way to keep him connected to the Southwest and Chicana/o cultures; they also kept him connected to a larger affect or identification known as *latinidad*—a pan-Latina/o connection that in turn enabled him to continually cross and re-cross borders so that he might find community in North Carolina.

Mario's sense of community was strengthened by the estrangement he felt from whites and African Americans who read his heightened performance of identity as foreign:

> I had *NEVER*
> *ever* experienced ANY animosity
> with *ANYONE* of color
> so then
> I come to the SOUTH
> and I like feel it
> for the FIRST time,
> but it was also in the South
> that I was able to like … identify with
> working class whites
> because I really had
> *nobody*
> to identify with.
> You know?
> And even some of the black students,
> yeah they were of color
> and they understood issues of color,
> and like we both knew
> what it was like to run into a cop at night
> as men of color
> but at the same time
> they were from very wealthy families.
> They were from very different backgrounds.
> They were from traditional Southern households
> where race
> is treated in a very different way.

The estrangement Mario describes is located along social and class lines, but he also spoke about feeling "forever foreign"—a feeling Nakayama describes well: "This is my country and my home, even if I do not look 'all-American'" (17). Mario's feelings of disillusionment and disidentification were further illuminated as he described his interactions with people outside the university:

One time I went to the bookstore to pick up my books
and this one woman said,
"Oh my God, where are you from?"
I was like … "Los Angeles."
"Oh, really
 you have such a great accent."
(In a thick Southern accent.)
And she had this *thick thick* Southern accent.
She was like,
"I just love your accent."
(Laughing.)
And I started laughing
it was ridiculous
and she said,
"I wish I had one"

Mario's story demonstrates the pervasiveness of dominant discourses that continue to position Latina/os as Others. Evident in this narrative is the way Mexican and Mexican American identities are conflated and how they are denied citizenship by their continually being positioned as outsiders or Others. This positioning serves to write over troubled histories in the United States such as the seizure of Southwestern states after the Treaty of Guadalupe Hidalgo in 1848, which essentially changed peoples' citizenship and rights overnight. For example, Inda writes that the treaty stipulated that the political rights of those in the ceded territory be the same as those of white citizens; however, Mexicans, being *mestizos*, were granted disparate privileges on the basis of the way they were racialized as either white or Indian, which in turn created images of foreignness.

The discursive practice of continually fashioning Mexicans as migrants or newly arrived erases the very real fact that Mexicans lived in what is now known as the United States before its seizure. These speech acts mirror strategies of manifest destiny through their multiple layers of erasure. This type of rhetorical strategy was also prominent during the 1999–2000 media-constructed "Latin Invasion/Explosion," which continued to position Latina/os, even those born in the United States, as trying to "cross over" into cultures in which they had no part. This Otherness was also heightened through the use of sexual imagery, particularly in the case of Ricky Martin, who was featured on the cover of one magazine with a bubble coming out of his mouth with the words "There's a Latin explosion in my pants" (Delgado and Calafell 239).

The stereotyping of Mexicans as forever foreign is similar to the experiences of Asian Americans in the United States. As Chan writes,

> The history of Asians in America can be fully understood only if we regard them as both immigrants and members of non-white minority groups. As immigrants many of their struggles resemble those that European immigrants have faced, but as people of non-white origins bearing distinct physical differences they have been perceived as "perpetual foreigners" who can never be completely absorbed into American society and its body politic. (187)

This continual sense of Otherness or exoticism has been well written about in the works of postcolonial scholars such as Anzaldúa, Hall, Fanon, and Said. In addition to the issues of appearances and the way they serve as markers of Otherness is the economics of Otherness and the ways Latina/o domestics and agricultural workers are rendered as objects or Others at the service of the dominant culture. These images then tend to be naturalized in popular culture through characters such as Rosario, the Latina maid in the popular sitcom *Will and Grace*.

As Jennings writes, the idea of Latina/os as Other runs deep in society, as evidenced by statements such as "Remember the Alamo." Tying Latina/o identities back to Native Americans, Jennings argues that it is ironic and contradictory for anyone to position Latina/os as Other. Similarly, Drzewiecka and Halualani in their exploration of Polish and Hawaiian diasporas write, "Diasporas of indigenous peoples are framed as oppositional contradictions; to be indigenous is to always be rooted in the land. To be removed from the land presupposes an 'unnatural' and 'foreign' displacement, or the eventual development of a Westernized (or American) identity. How can one arguably be of the Hawaiian nation without residing on 'aina land?" (353–354). Their essay also highlights the ways that people in the diaspora are Othered through the resignification of land by dominant groups.

This Otherness also occurs through the use of language as a marker of difference. Furthermore, as Anzaldúa writes in her discussion of linguistic terrorism, "Wild tongues can't be tamed, they can only be cut out" (76). Language, a central aspect of Mario's identity, becomes both a source of pride and a marker of difference that alienates him in North Carolina. Language, a necessary part of his identity, continues to mark him as Other, as does his physical appearance, which he labels as that of a "stereotypical Mexican." Language as a synecdoche for culture becomes the site where battles are played out. It oftentimes becomes the line that marks cultural assimilation or resistance. The

way that language is used, as a tool to demarcate difference, is illustrated in
another story Mario shares:

> So I was like
> you know
> that was another moment.
> This other time
> I was standing at Peabody
> it was raining
> and I was like
> oh my God
> how am I gonna get home
> because I had walked.
> And then
> all of a sudden this woman
> out of the blue says,
> "Oh I can give you a ride home."
> I was like,
> who is this white woman, right?
> So I said fuck it,
> I'll take the ride.
> So we went to her car
> and then she started asking me all these questions
> about,
> she worked at the hospital,
> and
> she's like, "How come Latinos,
> they're there like an hour before their appointment
> and they bring all their kids?"
> Asking me all these really stupid questions,
> right?
> And like when she dropped me off
> she said,
> "How many years have you been speaking English?"
> She said,
> "You have a pretty good vocabulary."
> An … I just remember I turned around
> and told her,
> "I told you I was born in Los Angeles
> didn't I?"
> And she's like,
> "Oh you did?"
> So apparently she was only listening to whatever she wanted,
> right?

And she said,
"Oh how long did it take you to learn English?"
"Well since kindergarten,
but I don't
remember."
It was obvious that she was not listening.
It was not registering.
She had already made ideas and then because
I looked like
the stereotypical Mexican
I mean that happens to me
all the time.

Mario's description of the event, specifically the way he notes that he looks like a stereotypical Mexican, coupled with the woman's insistence that he had only recently acquired English, again reaffirms the multiple ways that Latina/os are Othered in North Carolina. They continue to be named by others and discourses outside of their own control. The image of the stereotypical Mexican as being "brown" and forever foreign serves to reaffirm the "naturalness" of English speakers (read "white") in the space while highlighting the transitory or "unnatural" nature of Latina/os.

Writing about discourses of immigration, specifically around California's Proposition 187, Ono and Sloop note,

> Because one cannot see the difference between a "legal" Chicana or Chicano and an "illegal" Mexicana or Mexicano, the media environment in effect helps create a situation in which all Mexican-descent people are under suspicion as "other." … Thus, the right for Chicanos and Chicanas to be in the United States, let alone be members of the U. S. citizenry, is challenged. (17)

These dominant discourses that conflate Mexicans with Mexican Americans strategically deny the difference within and between these communities. Thus, we have cases such as the one described earlier where Mario is subjected to what Conquergood would term the enthusiast's infatuation, a superficial fascination or a desire for fetish ("Performing As a Moral Act"). Of this enthusiast's infatuation Conquergood writes, "Those of us in this performative stance will never permit the other 'to come before us as a radically different life form that rises to call our own form of life into question and to pass judgment on us, and through us, on the social formation in which we live.' Superficiality suffocates self as well as other" (7). Some might argue that the woman was making gestures toward understanding in her questions and because she offered to give Mario a ride; however, regardless of whether this is a beginning, Mario's comfort and self-esteem are still sacrificed so that those in power have the opportunity to "learn." Mario is responsible for educating the dominant cultures about difference rather than putting the burden back on them. Perhaps the woman could have really listened to what Mario was saying, or she could have educated herself in other ways about Mexican and Mexican American populations.

Mario Returns Home: The Music Almost Makes Me Forget …

He glanced her way as they drove through the darkness
with the music moving their spirits.
His words matching the rhythm,
"The music almost makes me forget.
 I can feel like we're not even here."
 She looked into his eyes,
the eyes that reminded her of home.
Through the song they had found Aztlán
and each time they sang it aloud to one another
 it was like they were there.
     The Southwest.
Still and always Mexico.
Having recently returned from Arizona,
he looked at her
with a smile on his face,
"And then when I got into the desert
I started thinking about you."
But on this last trip
the lure of the desert had been too much.
He was leaving.
How ironic that it was
her home
that seduced him away from North Carolina
back to LA.

This meditation highlights the fleeting and transitory nature of what we consider home. Home in this case is not something concrete; rather, it is concretized in the performance of memories associated with home. Home is the performative process of desire. It is the memories that create home. Similar to Peréz, who argues that Chicana/os are diasporic citizens, the poem draws upon the unifying myth of Aztlán as well as the nostalgia for the physical geography that marks the difference of the Southwest—the desert. The nostalgia for the stark barrenness of the desert becomes the signifier of home—the thing that cannot be resisted. The desert, not ever mentioned as central to his own experience, only important to mine, becomes a shared property through our stories—one that eventually calls him back home. The desert and its ability to draw Mario away from the South bear witness to the power of stories to blend together in ways that form communal property, defying ownership, much as in the novel *The Greatest Performance*. The characters in the novel share stories and interject each another into them so that the stories become shared and unifying, enabling spaces of resistance and survival. My stories of the Southwest and Mario's stories of the Southwest became *our stories*; thus, Mario's decision to draw upon the desert as a trope for return was not surprising.

I include Mario's narrative of his final trip to the Southwest, the trip that led to his decision to move home. Initially I was to accompany him on this trip, but at the last minute chose not to go because of work constraints. However, after he returned from the trip, I always wondered whether my presence would have made a difference in the decision. Would the physical reminder of our community have changed any of his decisions? These questions will never be answered. Here I include Mario's description of his decision to leave North Carolina:

> This time that I went back,
> because I go back and forth
> a lot,
> I was really tired.
> I had just taken my comps.
> I was just
> *really out of it.*
> I couldn't even hold conversations.
> And I was kinda like …
> not as thrilled
> because I had to present at the NACCS[2] conference
> and I *hadn't* written the paper
> and I was just thinking,
> "Man
> *what am I doing to myself?"*
> And then I have to drive back

and then go to Seattle …
But anyhow I got there …
and as soon as I got there
I was like oh my God …
it kinda felt good …
all the cars.
You know,
I told my dad,
kinda teasing,
"You know it's really nice
over there
with the trees and all that,
but you know I come here
and see the traffic
and it looks *beautiful* to me."
So I went and got my haircut right away
and went running
then I packed up the next day
and left
and I drove off.
At then *when I got into the desert*
I started thinking about
YOU.
I started to see all the Saquaro cactus,
and then
Phoenix,
and the
mountains.
All the stuff you talk about
and then
driving down to Tucson
and then
being in that
space.
You know
that space was transformed
into a
Chicano space.
You know?
And being surrounded by all these people.
And yeah,
people perform identities
but it was just so …
beautiful

that people have *those options*.
Women were running around with woven shirts
rebozos,
blouses,
and men wearing huaraches and gubayeras.
It was the space for it,
you know what I mean?
And even if people were performing
where else do you get that liberty?
It was just beautiful.
I felt like *ALL* the different parts of my world
came together.
LikeICouldBeAGradStudentICouldBe …
Chicano,
I could be … You know …
I could speak
Spanish,
I could speak
English.
You know what I mean?
I was interested
in what people were talking about in their presentations,
and
I LOVED IT! I LOVED IT.
It was great.
I had such a great time.
And umm
(*Pause.*)
I don't know,
I mean I can't even tell you how it felt.
Being in that space …
Being at the conference.
Being in a space
that was
explicitly Chicano,
but at the same time
a space
where I could be myself
and
all my different selves.
A space where
I could be
the academic presenting the paper,
I could be

the Chicano watching the performances.
Everything
It was the geography
because
you could *smell the desert air.*
I mean it was so dry
and
you know
I loved
it.
You could smell the desert air,
I mean you could walk outside and
see the sand.
'Cause you know
you walk down the
sidewalk
and instead of
lawn
there is
sand.

Mario's description of the conference of the National Association for Chicana and Chicano Studies in Tucson, Arizona, in the Southwest, again demonstrates the importance of geography in shaping identity for him. It is somewhat ironic that Mario's decision took place not only within the Southwest but at a Chicana/o studies conference. The excesses and spillages of the sites were immense. Was the excess overwhelming for him? Was this excess something Mario had not felt since he moved to North Carolina? The excesses and its performative possibilities were both overpowering and intoxicating. Not only does the Southwest birth and encourage Chicana/o identities, but (as Mario continually states in his narrative, "I could be … I could be …") it demonstrates the politics of possibility that exist within its spaces. The Southwest had more performative options for Mario than North Carolina, perhaps because of the long history of the land in relationship to Chicana/o and Mexican peoples. Mario could draw upon a myriad of scripts, moving in and out of them with ease at his leisure. In our experiences it seemed as if at that moment in time the South, specifically North Carolina, did not permit these identities, as they have yet to be realized—and may never be realized—in that space. Chicana/o identities could be realized only through performance and the communities it produced, but on larger scales these identities are still not understood or recognized by dominant cultures. Such a historically contingent and a land-based identity may never exist. If North Carolina is home to immigrants from Mexico who have yet to really realize a mature Mexican American generation, will Chicana/o identities ever emerge? Will new identities emerge, and what will they look like? Interestingly, though Mario names this space specifically as a Chicano space, it sounds very similar to Anzaldúa's description of the borderlands and *mestiza* identity as developing a tolerance for ambiguity. Ideally, Anzaldúa argues,

> The new mestiza copes by developing a tolerance for contradictions, a tolerance for ambiguity. She learns to be an Indian in Mexican culture, to be Mexican from an Anglo point of view. She learns to juggle cultures. She has a plural personality, she operates in a pluralistic mode—nothing is thrust out, the good the bad and the ugly, nothing abandoned. Not only does she sustain contradictions, she turns the ambivalence into something else. (*Borderlands* 101)

With this tolerance for ambiguity, the ability to cross multiple borders, and operate from a pluralistic mode, the *mestiza* should be able to exist in any place because, as Anzaldúa writes, home is transitory—it is what one carries with one (*Borderlands*). Thus, Mario's desire to not continue to sustain a Chicano identity outside of the Southwest, and his subsequent return to California illustrates the inhospitable nature of North Carolina in relation to what Mario describes as his experience. Thus, there must be an alternative identification that responds to the changing situation.

I in no way mean to suggest that the South exists as a monolithic Other force that overpowered Mario, giving him no option other than to leave. Instead, I am intent on conveying the sense of homelessness that seemed to guide many of our experiences as the weight of the history of the South bore down on our daily lives. Mario was always of the opinion that he would leave the South for the Southwest; thus, exercising his choice to leave was an act of agency. We had performed *Chicanismo* in the South, defying the history of the space by opening up possibilities for *latinidad* in our own small ways, even if they were not completely recognized by those around us. These performances were acts of resistance for us.

Describing his revelation that he no longer wanted to live in North Carolina, that it was necessary to leave this space and return to the geography and the homeland, Mario stated:

> The border
> is the border
> where it is marked

the presence of it expands.
I *feel* the border
in North Carolina now
… sometimes,
but of course
it's a different geography …
this geography kind of reminds me of where my parents are
from in Mexico.
But that's not my home.
So it was all that …
and then on the way home
we were still all happy
and singing
and we had breakfast in Phoenix.
And then when we crossed the border
into California
we
all of a sudden it got
real quiet.
And then
it got all quiet for like
half an hour.
And then somebody asked,
"What's it like in North Carolina?"
And I was like
"Oh, I don't know …"
And I got really kind of sad
'cause I thought,
"Oh shit!
I'm leaving *again.*"
I'm like,
"It's *alright*
when I first got there it was
horrible
and
I hated it.
I thought I was going to die and kill myself.
You know … slowly
you get *used* to it
and then you know it becomes
alright."
And then it got *all quiet* for like five minutes
and then someone said,
"Isn't it sad that such a

> horrible place
> can actually become an okay place
> to live when you get
> *used to it?"*
> And it just got to me.
> That just stuck in my mind.
> That just totally stuck in my mind
> and
> like I decided
> thinking about it for days
> and
> not
> long after that I decided
> *I was leaving.*
> And now …
> I'm going *home.*

Mario's narrative resonates with Boym's discussion of diasporic intimacy as a punctuation. Boym argues, "Just as one learns to live with alienation and reconciles oneself to the uncanniness of the world around and to the strangeness of the human touch, there comes a surprise, a pang of intimate recognition, a hope that sneaks in through the back door, punctuating the habitual estrangement of everyday life" (229). In this case Mario's sense of being content with his displacement, accepting it as a "normal" part of his everyday experience, was challenged by a glimmer of hope, a punctuation that very tangibly reminded him of what he was missing, and he could no longer go back.

Conclusions

I have offered a glimpse. Too often when we think of the realm of Chicana/o studies we do not move beyond the Southwest, despite the demographic figures that tell us it would be wise to do so. Within diaspora studies there is a paucity of literature addressing the unique situations of Chicana/os living both in and out of a conquered homeland simultaneously, not completely diasporic. I hope this work begins to fill some of the existing gaps in the literature. I have argued that in spaces of new regional convergences and migrations, particularly between Mexican Americans, Chicana/os, and Mexicans, there are multiple border crossings, constituting transcultural exchanges that defy existing discourses that separate these groups in traditionally populated areas such as the Southwest. Borders are crossed and re-crossed in new ways that defy static and essentialist notions of what it means to be Chicana/o, Mexican, and Mexican American. The lines are blurred and communities are formed that cross nationality, economics, and region. Inda has described the relationship between history, discourse, and place and the ways in which they inform and create fluid performative identities. Similarly, I have expanded Inda's descriptions of racial performativity by examining the ways that diasporic individuals perform and create community as the diaspora expands within the nation-state, challenging preexisting ideas of home and homelands. Specifically, I have located these movements through the identification of three themes: *Yo Soy Chicano y Mexicano*, which examines the ways that Mario acknowledges and bridges the tensions between Chicana/os and Mexicana/os to gain a larger identification and community; *A Case of Diasporic Intimacy: "You Are My Chicano Space"* examines the ways in which Mario holds on to the rhetoric of *Chicanismo* and the Southwest while maintaining his connection to Mexican immigrant communities; and *Forever Foreign: A Stereotypical Mexican* demonstrates the ways in which Mario's interaction with other communities, African American and white, strengthened his connection to Mexican community through an affect of foreignness. I followed each of these themes with Mario's narrative of his decision to return to the West. Each of these themes sheds light on the migrations that continue to change the face of the South.

Though I have offered only a glimpse of what is happening in the South, I hope this glimpse will continue the conversation about the changing face of the South and the role Latinos are playing in it. I have raised questions regarding the necessity of new political identifications that speak to pan-Latina/o and cross-generational groups. Perhaps for the first time there can truly be cross-Latina/o social movements because of the rise in connections and migrations. The relevance of these convergences for us as performance scholars lies in the ways performances of excess and identity make these connections possible. As places such as the South continue to change, we also need to challenge our assumptions about race and identity, perhaps beginning to embrace truly new and unique convergences and spaces of coming together.

· 3 ·

LOOKING FOR MARINA/LOOKING FOR MYSELF: A CHICANA FEMINIST PERFORMANCE

"I do not re-write history. I tell the story for the first time. The story of holding one's self apart, to hold oneself together."

(Moraga *Loving in the War Years* 202)

"I am, however, caught in the time lag between the colonial and the postcolonial, in a decolonial imaginary reinscribing the old with the new."

(Pérez 127)

"Activism is an engagement with the hauntings of history, a dialogue between the memories of the past and the imaginings of the future manifested through the acts of our own present yearnings. It is an encounter with the ghosts that reside within and inhabit the symbolic and geographic spaces that shape our worlds."

(Rodríguez *Queer Latinidad* 37)

Reflections on Preparations for a Journey

I prepare to return to a home that I do not know but that continues to define me. Mexico City awaits me. Here I will come face to face with the women of my cultural past—Marina, Guadalupe, Frida. Do they wait for me? Do they long for my return as I long for the comfort I will find in the shadows and remnants of their lives? You lose your home, you lose your culture, you lose your father ... then what do you have? Where do you go and what do you do? You must reinvent yourself, I suppose. Reinvent yourself in the space you long ago decided to shut yourself off from. But when you are empty what choice do you have?

Looking over Lonely Planet's guide to Mexico City I feel somewhat peculiar. I note John Noble's cautionary words that "some indigenous peoples have learned to mistrust outsiders after five centuries of exploitation. They don't like being gawked at by tourists and can be very sensitive about cameras: if in doubt about whether it's OK to take a photo, always ask first" (36–37). How lucky I am to have John Noble to teach me manners and reintroduce me to Mexico, though its history is written on my body. Am I a tourist seeking a "journey from an everyday situation to an extraordinary location"? (Edensor 105). I have been a tourist before, *la guera* who could so easily pass. I remember being so envious as I spoke to a friend in North Carolina whose parents are Scottish–Irish and Mexican when she described her experience of crossing the border and feeling at home. Her ability to blend in was an experience I was not privy to, yet desired. Her journey, my futile desire for authenticity, it all came so simply for her. I wanted that simplicity. I wanted that sense of purity.

I had been a tourist. The woman who had journeyed to Nogales, right before coming to North Carolina, in search of souvenirs that would somehow "authenticate" her identity in North Carolina—the Mexican blankets, the posters, and all other things that she proudly displayed in her room (Calafell "Disrupting the Dichotomy"). These items held memories; these souvenirs symbolized her identity (J. Gonzalez; Love and Kohn). *You've reduced yourself to a picture you hang on the wall. You gaze at me looking for meaning and self-worth, but I am not simply an object to be gazed upon; I am much more visceral.* These were things she had never really owned even at home in Phoenix, but somehow in North Carolina they were essential. Performance artist Carmelita Tropicana once said that she felt like a tourist returning to her home country of Cuba (Troyano). I understand what she means as I ask, "Who am I going to this place that hides traces of identity?" Maybe I am something worse than a tourist? Am I a wannabe anthropologist who is unenlightened and is looking for that exotic Other that is myself? Will I go to Mexico as I did before looking for souvenirs to authenticate my identity? Souvenirs that are foreign to me that I somehow still deem essential? Is this simply an uncritical nostalgia embodied in souvenirs?

Loss of culture; loss of home; loss of family. So many layered losses and what do you have but the condition of the exile. The exile is estranged from so much all at once. The exile longs for authenticity. *But what is that?* In the poem "Elena," Pat Mora tells the story of a Mexican woman who has immigrated to the United States. As her children become Americanized she becomes more and more embarrassed by her lack of English skills. Now I am in a similar position as I enter Mexico City, much like Rosario Morales writing of returning to Puerto Rico: "This is not home. I'll always be clumsy with the language, always resentful of the efforts to remake me, to do what my parents couldn't manage" (as qtd. in Behar 150). Home: what does it mean when you have lost everything, and how ironic is it for me to claim a home that I have never known except in the faint, faint memories of distant relatives or our imagined realities of life in the old country? Like Ruth Behar, who compares being in a diasporic situation to experiencing loss or mourning, "I come to feel, deeply, the enormous sorrow of being countryless, the enormous rage of being countryless. And I also experience the other side of this: the enormous sorrow of having too much country, the enormous rage of having nothing but *patria*" (142). The rage of having nothing but *patria* is all I have.

In her book *Remembering Cuba: Legacy of a Diaspora*, Andrea O'Reilly Herrera interviews Cuban American exiles about their experiences growing up displaced. Herrera writes, "Their exile consciousness, therefore, can be attributed both to the physical proximity of Miami to the Island, and to the fact that they were socialized in a socioeconomic environment that reinforces a particularly strong sense of Cuban cultural identity. As a result, quite a few pointed out that when they are in Miami, they never have to think about their identities" (xxiii). I never think about my identity when I am in Arizona; Aztlán is such a luxury. But in this space of North Carolina I must constantly face it, as I am deemed both authentic and inauthentic. My Spanish skills and my white skin mark me as inauthentic to Mexican immigrants and non-Latina/o Latin Americanists who have been deemed experts of "Latin" culture. I am reminded of the words of a well-meaning friend who commented, "Well I think the way you speak Spanish is sort of representative of your identity, you know all the symbols and the order but when you speak it, it doesn't sound quite right … But it doesn't matter 'cause you know all the symbols and the order, you just have a problem articulating it." *You are an imposter.* His statement, so telling of all my inadequacies and insecurities, rang true in my flushed cheeks and embarrassed eyes. How would I speak? How would I perform as I entered the space of Mexico City, the site of *mestiza* birth? *You come now looking for answers, but it's not that easy. You must meet me halfway.*

Fast Forward: Embarking on a Pilgrimage

Travelers worldwide make pilgrimages to La Basilica de Nuestra Senora de Guadalupe in Mexico City, the spot where La Virgen was said to have appeared to the villager Juan Diego on Mount Tepeyac. On this spot is the original church built after the Virgin's appearance, as well as several other churches. Pilgrims come from far and wide to walk or climb on their knees up the hill to the church. Others stand on the moving sidewalk to catch glimpses of the image of the Virgin, which is said to be the original item that appeared on Juan Diego's cloak when he opened it for disbelievers. Though this was on my list of places to venture to in Mexico City, it was not my priority. Rather, my desire was with *her*—Malintzin. I went to the Basilica and saw Guadalupe and felt nothing. I was not moved by her image; instead I was moved by my feelings of nothingness, my numbness. I was moved by the emotions and beliefs of other pilgrims who cried in her presence. The uneventfulness of it all surprised me. *Your irreverence is so blatant. Your desire is blasphemous. Your jealousy, desire for feeling, desire for passion, and need for reconciliation are all so transparent ... too bad they're not for her. They are misplaced and I have become your space of renewal. Accept your fate.* Maybe it was because I felt so close to her because of my own sense of loss. Maybe it was because I suddenly felt like a woman who was free, taking things into her own hands for the first time. My marriage, just days before, was both liberating and constraining, as I no longer knew exactly who I was. *You are a woman in the middle.* Una mujer mala *who has symbolically turned her back on her family through the "sin" of self-indulgence, yet is always tempted by guilt and the desire for affirmation.* My journey was, as rhetorical scholar Carole Blair writes of those who make journeys to memorial sites, a physical labor (46). It was a labor of love …

Reflections in a Dream

I am dreaming in bright colors of a Preconquest past that is somehow mine and yet not mine. I am dreaming of her face. Her plain wide face, her full lips, and her long dark hair have come to me in visions time and time again, yet now they are so blaringly clear that I can no longer ignore them. A tear gently glides down the side of her cheek and my first impulse is to lean over and kiss it, but instead I wipe it away with my tongue. Her tears spoke so much as I tasted their bitter-sweetness on my tongue. I look into her eyes and for a second there is silence. She lifts her hand to gently caress my face and pull me closer to her. She pushes my hair behind my ear and whispers,

"*Mijita, where have you been? All this time I have called your name and not once have you answered? I have longed for you to come back to me.*"

The voices whispering all along, were they hers? Were they mine or someone else's?

The ghost of Malintzin Tenépal has been banging on my door again. Or could she be disguising herself as our comadre, *La Llorona the wailing woman, searching for her lost children and culture? I am reminded of the words of Sarah Amira De La Garza, who spoke about the power of the shapeshifter and the power of Chicanas as translators. I guess we all get used to wearing different masks at different times. Malinalli, Marina, Malintzin, I long to know you, but all I know are vague descriptions of you from a book written by a Spaniard. Marina, I want to feel your flesh. I first fell in love with you in 1995. I remember you. Do you remember me? Yes, good Mexican Catholic girl suddenly being reawakened from a comfortable malaise, being led astray into a world of sex, colonialism, and religious critique. Transplanted from a life of certainties to a life of questions with no immediate answers, out came an angry, feisty, ambiguous Chicana who suddenly became the black sheep of her family with all her radical views and "selfishness." Yes, you and I go way back, but lately it seems like we have been so out of touch. Of course, there is the picture hanging on the wall. Right above Lupe's. Now isn't that ironic! For once you are above her.*

I admit, Marina, I only came back to you out of necessity. It was not because I heard your voice. I wanted to talk about colonialism and of course there you were. How can you talk about colonialism and not talk about me? Of course not, though it sure seems like so many other scholars have tended to overlook Mexicanas and Chicanas when they want to talk about (post)colonialism, as if our theories and experiences have no value. Perhaps we have no cultural capital? I remember why I had fallen in love with you in the first place. You represent so much to me. Imagine a woman not afraid of her sexuality. Imagine a woman who had the power to create a new people. Imagine the woman who was my mother, who was my lover, who was everything to me. And now I return with the question Cherríe asked, "What kind of lover have you made me mother?"[1]

I wonder, what did you do when Hernan, your lover (or was he your tool?), married you off to one of his men because his "proper" Spanish wife was coming into YOUR world? Did you laugh? Did you cry? Or did you make love to Juan Jarmillo[2] *in a vengeful passion to spite Hernan so he would hear the cries and know exactly what he was missing? I ask you, Marina, because I need you and I need to know. Did you long for his body even after he left? Did you curse the day you met him? What did you do? You created the culture I have lost and I need you to bring me back. Marina, what about your mother who sold you off so that your brother might fare better? You know all about betrayal by love and loss: Tracionado Por Amor. My lover, my mother, my sister, I need you more than ever …*

Marina, I come to you now because, honestly, I see that you and I are in the same boat. We have both lost our voices. Yours has been missing for such a long time and, believe me, lots of us have been trying to help you find it. For me it started to happen in the fall of 2000 when I left Aztlán. It continued seven months later when I lost tata, my grandfather, my father, my guardian, my heart, my soul, my culture. With him went my connection to Aztlán and any sense of self and cultural knowledge I had ever known. So now here I am looking for a story, looking for my story and all I can see is you. Chicana feminists such as Adelaida del Castillo, Norma Alarcón, Lucha Corpi, and Carmen Tafolla have all tried to reclaim your narrative from those machistas such as Octavio Paz who call you a whore when they compare you to Guadalupe. Listen, hija, I did not sell out my people. When they call you a whore and cast Guadalupe as a virgin they leave us no other options because as Chicanas we are all stuck. I am not a virgin; I am not a whore. I am a woman without a voice who perhaps really never had a voice to call her own. The story of who I am is lost and now I need your help to find it. How can anyone understand the complexity of your life and your decisions? They can't, and it all comes out very one-dimensionally. You need to speak; your narrative needs to be heard. You need self-definition right now just as much as I do. I am hoping in my journey toward you, I will also find my voice and perhaps this pilgrimage, this performance in which I engage, can add to a Chicana feminist project of bringing your narrative to life because it is so embodied, because it is so performed. Thus, Marina, I ask you to let me work through my pain, my loss, my own experiences of nothingness and reclaim or find my narrative with you as I look for yours. Can this cultural pilgrimage give testimony not only to the cultural, but also to the personal in ways that show how Chicanas are deeply affected by the cultural narratives that dictate the proper roles of women and in a sense deprive us not only of your voice, but also ours? That's right; this is about more than just me. Can you help me find my way back? If I perform and honor your memory in a space that refuses to officially recognize it, can WE free ourselves? Can we rewrite our narratives?

In the City …

I am looking for Malintzin, but she is nowhere to be found. I see small glimpses of her in the faces of people in the crowds in the city, in my mirror, and in a mural in the National Palace, but this is not enough. I need more than these pieces—much, much more. I am exhausted, overwhelmed, and driven by my desire for reconciliation (Doxtader "Reconciliation"). My furtive search, my desire, my anticipation are all manifesting themselves in my desperate hunt for knowledge of her. Books have been read over and over again. Poems have been devoured for clues, and now, in a sign of our times, the Internet has been searched. If only I could find her then perhaps I could find myself. Finally, there it is: the address and the space I have longed for—her home, *our home. You are close. So very close. Cuidado amor.* Chicana feminist Gloria Anzaldúa writes that as Chicanas we are turtles, meaning that we carry our homes on our backs. When does this transitory home become too heavy? Have I found what Sandra Cisneros gestures toward in *The House on Mango Street?* Is this a real home or a space to call my own? A room of my own?

The house in Coyoacán built by Hernan Cortés is where he allegedly killed his wife Catalina, who had come from Cuba (Caistor; Krauss; Noble). The bright red house, Casa Colorada, is a private residence located quietly across from a park a little farther down from a market (Krauss; Noble). Unlike the multiple official public spaces bearing the name, words, or reminders of Hernan Cortés, this house was unmarked and unassuming. I had once heard from a local that a statue of Marina, Cortés, and a lion stood in the park across the street from the house, until it had to be destroyed because of the neighbors found it distasteful. Nothing gave away the house's illustrious history or a clue of its former resident except perhaps, in a clichéd fashion, the passionate red of the house. *Aren't all of us Latinas associated with red?* In an article from *The New York Times*, the owner of the house, muralist Rina Lazo, explains the private nature of the house: "For Mexico to make this house a museum, would be like the people of Hiroshima creating a monument for the man who dropped the atomic bomb … We're not malinchistas, but we want to conserve Mexican history" (Krauss). Lazo's words echoed the words of a storeowner in La Zona Rosa who explained to me when my companion and I searched for items that depicted Malintzin that she was important to Spanish history not Mexican history. *They say you are buried in Spain while Hernan lies in this soil? Is it true?* A few streets away from Casa Colorada, Casa Azul, the home of Frida Kahlo, is open to the public. A public memorial, a private shame, Mexican history, the value of women, and public shame are all played out within a few miles in Coyoacán as Malintzin exists in a complex space of absence and presence. As Blair, Jeppeson, and Pucci note, monuments "instruct" their visitors about what should be valued in the future and the past (350). The fact that Malintzin's house remains unmarked and unendorsed again attests to the way that Malintzin is devalued in the writing of history. Furthermore, Blair notes that memorial sites by their very existence create communal spaces (48). Thus, conversely, we must ask what does the lack of memorialization signify?

The Heart of the Matter: Mourning for Marina

A woman who was my lover, my mother, my sister.
Blood, sacrifice, life.
A woman who was my lover, my mother, my sister.
Seeing beyond your time, looking ahead while
looking back.
A woman who was my lover, my mother, my sister.
Looking for a face, but there is none.
What does it mean? All I see is a shoulder.
A shoulder of a man who hid your face.
Mixing blood,
opening yourself not as *La Chingada*,
but as the true creator you were.
A woman who was my lover, my mother, my sister.
A woman who has no tears, somehow they are all
that I seem to have now.
Displaced, misplaced, misunderstood.
Tears fall from my eyes because of my lack of vision
compared to all that you could foresee.
A woman who was my lover, my mother, my sister.
Malinalli

(Mexico City, May 22, 2002, 5:30 p.m.)

In cultures that seem to value or idealize sacrifice (through images of the virgin) and recognize the relevance of blood (in the multiple images of the bloody Christ and through the narratives told of Aztec sacrifice), Malintzin's place in national and cultural memory is uncertain and contested because of her blood sacrifice, her blood mixing, and her sexuality. *Hija, do you remember the heat you received for that assertion? Yet you refused to let it go and you refused to let me burn.* Malintzin's absence may be reflective of Stavans' observation that "unlike men, Hispanic women are indeed forced to open up. And they are made to pay for their openness" (230). Her existence as scapegoat or representative of blood mixing may be so abject because purity is such a valued concept held up by an unrealistic ideal: the Virgin of Guadalupe. *Psst ... Oh, mijita, yet another one, you were disciplined for that one at that dissertation defense?*

Those "well-meaning" non-Latina/o Latin Americanists never let you off the hook. Was it a patriarchal order, racist, or other symbolic oppressive structure coming down on you then, just as it has for me over the countless years? Malintzin is forced to pay for her perceived openness by existing in a state of limbo, superficially present in national narratives, yet symbolically and literally faceless in the few visual renderings of this narrative throughout the city, such as Diego Rivera's *El Arribo De Hernan Cortés* in the National Palace. In this image painted in 1951 we see a blond, white-skinned Hernan Cortés with Malintzin trailing behind. She bows her head, hiding her face behind his shoulder and gun. The image reminds me of the writings of Stavans: "The primal scene of the clash with the Spaniards is a still-unhealed rape: the phallus, as well as gunpowder, was a crucial weapon used to subdue" (228–229). Could this be what we see reflected in this mural? All we see is the corner of Malintzin's left eye, her lips, black hair, and large bright blue hoop earring. She carries a large bundle with her left hand, and slung on her back is a child with bright blue eyes and tan skin— a *mestizo*, Martin. Cortés and Malintzin do not look our way; only Martin makes eye contact with the viewer. Where is her narrative? She has none; instead others write over her story with their narratives, fixing her in a virgin/whore dichotomy in national memory that she traverses only in the imaginations and memory performances of everyday citizens such as Susana, a woman I spoke with during my journey who had told me of her great love of Malintzin.

Limón has written about the relationships among desire, fantasy, and domination in colonial encounters and their representation in popular or mass culture. One prevalent trope is that of the white male and the Mexican girl, who is often cast as the self-sacrificing senorita. As observed by Keller, in film the self-sacrificing senorita often dies giving her life for her white lover so that in the end he can be with a white woman. Considering this ideal of sacrifice within the narrative of Malintzin, we might see her as serving as a sacrificial lamb of sorts in this history of colonialism. Like the self-sacrificing senorita, her narrative ends while that of her white lover continues. Pérez's argument about the Oedipal Conquest Triangle or Complex in which the Indian mother, Malintzin, is denigrated sheds light upon this situation:

> Precisely because Paz and others like him cannot come to terms with the Indian woman who, in their eyes, betrayed the race by embracing the white male colonizer. Yet contradictions proliferate. At some level he is compelled to embrace the colonizer father, Malinche becomes the dreaded phallic mother who will devour him, castrate him, usurp him of his own phallus/power. He must therefore ally with the white colonizer father, but to do so is to ally in ambivalence. (107)

This situation, Pérez argues, will continue to be played out over and over again as Malintzin continues to be despised as an abject object (107). Malintzin's lack of visibility in the city bears witness to this argument, as her name is whispered while Hernan Cortés' name and image are literally written across the city. *Yes, even on the wall of the museum of El Templo Mayor right next to the cathedral, his name is written.*

Although there is no marker for or museum in her home, many are aware of the house's presence. Try as they may to ignore her, they cannot stop history, because the absence of the past "'other' meanings haunts the presence of the material now" (Kuftinec 83). As Kuftinec asserts, "These absences, 'empty' spaces within the city, remain shadowed by spectres of what-was-before and possible-futures-to-come, both engaging in the politics of divisiveness within the city" (83). Mexican and Chicana/o identities cannot be limited by discourse, as "identity cannot, then, reside in the name you can say or the body you can see ... Identity is perceptible only through a relation to an other" (Phelan 13). *Our history is inescapable whether named or unnamed.*

The Pilgrimage Revisited ...

Naively we had journeyed to Coyoacán specifically with the intent of seeing Frida Kahlo's and Malintzin's houses, in the hope that they would somehow illuminate our understandings about the roles of Mexican women in past and present societies. Coyoacán is where Cortés and his men were said to have prepared for their attack on Tenochtitlán (Caistor 124). After he had taken over the city, Cortés remained in Coyoacán while his new palace was being built on the site of Moctezuma's palace. Taking the subway from the Zocolo, the historic district, to Coyoacán, we first ventured to Frida Kahlo's house, Casa Azul. After visiting Kahlo's house we began walking through the market in search of 57 Hidalgo, the only tangible connection we had to Malintzin. Anticipation was driving me crazy. *My heart is racing. I am scared. What will I find? Can I handle this right now? I am embarrassed by my desire and my need.* I had been imaging this moment since I had arrived in Mexico City. *I am waiting for you.* A strange sense of excitement and guilt rushed over me. *My presence is an intrusion, but I cannot stop. How many others have come into this space before me looking for a mythic Eve figure who was neither virgin nor whore, but a real fleshed woman whose story is so cloudy yet so familiar to me because of our perceived imperfections and shared losses?* Religious and cultural logic dictated that

I should have been more excited about going to see the shrine to the Virgin of Guadalupe, but this simply wasn't the case. *I'm sorry but you are nothing like her, you are a daughter in my own image and personality.* I was like a child asking the inevitable question on a road trip: "Are we there yet?" Much like those pilgrims I had seen venture toward the image of Guadalupe, an enormous sense of desire, hope, and reverence reverberated throughout my body. *Can she be my savior? Can she help me find my way back? Marina, I have lost my story, I have lost my voice, I have lost my culture. Can you help me recuperate them by my visit to this "blasphemous sacred" site?* Blair notes the affects that memorials have on the people who venture to see them. She asserts that touching them "yields profound responses" (46). My companions, somewhat taken aback by my reverence, remarked to me that perhaps I should remember Marina was a traitor, but it was too late—I was already seduced. *Self-knowledge and possibility are incredible sites of seduction; continue on don't let the voices stop you. Don't be disciplined again.*

Walking toward Casa Colorada, I felt her presence immediately. *Do you know I am here?* My blasphemy, her "sainthood," all played out. The black bars over each of the windows seemed to be a metaphor for the containment of Malintzin's story in national narratives. To the left of the house was a sign letting the passerby know the house is for sale. Who will bear the "burden" of ownership? Who will let her legacy live? At the time when we shot a picture, I did not notice the sign because I was struck by the unassuming nature of the house in a small hidden-away neighborhood a few blocks from the main market in the town. The ghosts of the past haunt as an eerie feeling comes over those who come near it.

The huge wood door had a large metal doorknocker that looked like a hand coming out of the mouth of an ominous creature. Much like a representation of my own feeling of being silenced or stunted, the hand was held back by the monster of history, by the force of narratives, official narratives of which we have always been defined. Now was the time for self-definition. *I touch the walls, and with each caress, my pleasure, my pain, my loss, all manifest themselves in welled-up tears.* Large windows that form a balcony leave me wondering, *Did you look over the burning city? Did you weep over the changing landscape? Over a lost love?* A weeping woman on a balcony overlooking the destruction her lover made across the land of her birth? What secrets did these walls hold? *Moments of seduction, joy, and finally betrayal are all to be found here in this moment of past, present, and future convergences.* This house is some distance from the National Palace and the Templo Mayor in the Zocolo district, where Cortés set up shop after he had disempowered Moctezuma. Was this the distance that Cortés purposely put between them? *There has been so much distance between us; is it because of the master narrative of your* mestiza *birth and the many "truths" you have been told about me? Passion, self-knowledge, and the pain of history are all around us.* The force of history, the force of memory past, present, and future, is inescapable as I stand on this sacred site. *Sacred is the site of mestiza birth.* This site where Cortés was said to have killed his wife is haunted by mysteries and unanswered questions. Unanswered questions allow the visitor to re-imagine, re-tell, and re-perform. Perhaps it is because this house remains unsanctioned that it is a place of renewal, allowing visitors to write their own histories and stories. What would official narratives deny? Standing near the house I merge my story into hers and our narratives become one. *We are not that different.* We reflect on one another, change one another, and now as I enter your space we are fused. *I have come home to you another mujer mala. No more mourning. The voice you lost was never your own. Those were not our words; they were only scripts we had been force-fed all along.* In this space, I create my own embodied understanding of my legacy, of my culture. All along I had been mourning the loss of my voice, culture, and story, not realizing that in this process, in this space of anticipation, and finally in this space of reclamation and reconciliation through the traversing of my past, present, and future, I have created a space of new possibilities, or what Pollock terms a possible real (*Telling Bodies*). As Corey writes, "Performance ethnography is one way of releasing suspended voices, building connections between the expression of a people and those people themselves, with power, possibility and integrity" ("On Possibility" 332). The possibility of remaking in the performance of language and in this the embodiment of history can be liberatory and intoxicating, as it is the ultimate seduction.

The Space of Possibility: Past, Present, and Future ...

Cherríe Moraga writes about being in love with the unrequited or simply being in love with the feeling of desire. Wanting to stay in that place of limbo yet not quite limbo, that place of possibility, can give a sense of extreme pleasure. Anticipation can be everything. Reversing things a bit, Michel Foucault argues that within homosexuality the most pleasurable part of sex is the "recollection rather than the anticipation of the act ... the homosexual imagination is for the most part concerned with reminiscing about the act rather than anticipating it" (297). This reminiscing or nostalgia creates a queer temporality that privileges memory because homosexual acts are prefigured as Other or outside of "master" narration. Leo Bersani argues that displacement, in this case the displacement of the act, is endemic to sexuality (221). Writing about the mobility of desire, Bersani argues that sexual desire initiates "an agitated fantasmatic activity in which original (but, from the start, unlocatable) objects of desire get lost in the images they generate" (221). Alan Sinfield elaborates on the idea of a queer temporality or anticipation by writing of a queer diaspora: "For coming out is not once-and-for-all … we never quite arrive" (118). Similarly, this space of unfulfilled desire might seem somewhat sadomasochistic or may rather exist as a byproduct of not just a queer desire, which Halperin defines as an identity at odds with the normal, but also the desire for "original" experience (which has been denied) that may be a product of a postcolonial or exile condition. So this space of what is unrequited exists as a space of nostalgia, a space that longs for what never was and will never be. Longing for a space that will never be, but enjoying the desire, "the exile is a person who having lost a loved one, keeps searching for the face he loves in every new face and, forever deceiving himself, thinks he has found it" (Arenas, qtd. in Herrera xxiv). Each of these sources contributes to what I term a queer temporality. Others such as Bell and Binnie, Sedgwick, and Altman raise questions about the possibility for a queer diaspora or nationality, based upon shared experience or feeling, but I turn to Foucault and other queer theorists as a means not to talk about sexuality but to talk about the feeling of being positioned outside of dominant narratives.

I cite this passage by Foucault because of the possibilities of where it can go theoretically, though I realize the possibility that it could provoke much critique. For example, Leo Bersani dismisses Foucault's statement by saying it directs attention to "romances of memory and the idealization of the presexual, the courting imagination" (220). My intention is not to employ this framework as if to suggest that those who employ a queer temporality have no history of their own, and thus must create history; rather, I argue that dominant discourses do in fact include them in narratives, but in ways that marginalize them, do not privilege their experiences, or allow them to define those experiences. Thus, they employ disidentificatory strategies such as memory and queer temporality to challenge these constructions and power interests, offer counter-narratives, and create communities based upon these feeling of difference and excess.

These personal narratives, Frederick Corey argues, disturb master narratives and rewrite them through their performative elements ("The Personal" 250). Personal narratives, renegotiated memories, may be born out of "a symptom of loss of grand narratives of a culture" and may be programs for "recuperating loss" (Cox "Cultural Memory" 9). Citing the work of Marcuse, who believed in the "liberating power of remembrance," J. Robert Cox argues that memory "has the potential to subvert one-dimensional consciousness and also to prefigure an alternative future" ("Memory, Critical Theory" 3). The argument from history "allows us, potentially, to transcend, or 'go beyond' the claims of presentist argument. It recovers, re-collects, and reassembles what has been 'left out' of public debate" (12). The tensions or paradoxes lie in the question of "how to become modern and to return to sources" and the "need to preserve the nucleus of a culture—its temporal identity—on one hand, and the need to break with reified interpretations of the past" (Cox "Cultural Memory" 4).

Taking Elin Diamond's discussion of performativity a step further, Alberto Sandoval-Sánchez and Nancy Saporta Sternbach note that beyond the doing and the thing done, performance points toward the future to give the audience a sense of expectation, a future perfect that will have been done (97). I liken this future perfect to D. Soyini Madison's performance of possibilities, which speaks to the ability of performed personal narrative to traverse margins and centers. Alberto Sandoval-Sánchez and Nancy Saporta Sternbach write, "To recover that past is to activate ethnic memory, a memory that, once recalled projects itself into a future performance of being, of selfhood. ... performance is not only a 'doing and a thing done,' but also a 'thing imagined,' a 'thing to be done,' a thing projected forward" (104). Thus, not only are present and past conditions effected in the performance or re-embodiment of memory, but in this telling the future is opened. Idealistically, these openings would allow for altered futures and possibilities, forays into materiality. Trauma to become susceptible to critique through its telling, this performance, this pilgrimage, enables a re-storied history that is activated in each step I take. Others such as Davis have examined the rhetoric of pilgrimage as a way to interrogate larger cultural histories, but the journey I take is very personal and explicitly linked to Malintzin. Guided by a Four Seasons of Ethnography perspective (Gonzalez "The Four Seasons"), performance ethnography perspective, or understanding art as meditation (De La Garza), I understand the importance of using personal experience, body knowledge, and reflection to bear upon my history and theorizations. Thus, I offer my own narrative, my own rewriting of the space, and my own story of mourning to re-perform possibilities for recuperating colonial narratives, specifically, the narrative of Malintzin, to offer possibilities for the future.

As I walk through the space of Mexico City, our stories becomes active with every step I take in search of her. Writing of the decolonial process, Frantz Fanon argues,

> The violence which has ruled over the ordering of the colonial world, which has ceaselessly drummed the rhythm for destruction of native social forms and broken up without reserve the systems of reference of the economy, the customs of dress and external life, that same violence will be claimed and taken over by the native at the moment when, deciding to embody history in his own person, he surges into the forbidden quarters. (40)

In the same way, pilgrimage and the desire to reimagine history and national memory are actions for those postcolonial subjects to embody history. Affect created through performances of queer temporality calls preexisting subjects into spaces of identification where lived experience is altered and potentialities are opened as identity continues to be in the making. Taking a cue from Erik Doxtader, whose work on South African reconciliation argues for a middle voice that actualizes what it explains, I identify performative process or pilgrimage as a means of honoring identities in the making and alternative forms of advocacy ("Making Rhetorical History"). Doxtader's study acknowledges reconciliation as a rhetorical process or procedure that is both action and object. In the same way I propose the study of memory and pilgrimage as spaces of affective performance that critiques and actualizes. The passivity and erasure Malintzin finds in the pages of Mexican philosophy, murals, and history books is shattered through the pilgrimage I make to her home to mourn not only for her but also for myself. Gloria Anzaldúa argues that a Chicana identity is grounded in a history of resistance and adds that "Aztec female rites of mourning were rites of defiance protesting the cultural changes which disrupted the equality and balance between male and female, and protesting their demotion to a lesser status, their denigration. Like *la Llorona*, the Indian woman's only means of protest was wailing" (*Borderlands* 21). Thus, I wail for myself, I wail for Malinalli, and I wail for other Chicanas.

PART II

THE STAGE WE CALL OUR LIVES:
PERFORMANCE AND THE MASS
CONSUMPTION OF LATINA/O
IDENTITIES

· 4 ·

MY LOVE/HATE RELATIONSHIP
WITH EL VEZ

Ricky Martin, Jennifer Lopez, Marc Anthony, Carlos Santana, El Vez. El Vez???
During the years 1998–2000 the entertainment industry in the United States
of America was rocked by the sound of Latin rhythms and moved by Latin
beats. The "Latin Invasion/Explosion" put the names of Ricky Martin, Marc
Anthony, and others on the lips of mainstream white middle-class consumers (Delgado and Calafell). Though these stars were celebrated for their mass
appeal or their abilities to "cross over" into the mainstream, discourses regarding affirmative action, immigration, and media stereotypes were still pervasive
and problematic. An affirmation/negation relationship became evident in the
popular press, where Latina/os were celebrated, but only in relation to their
value to please aesthetically or to entertain rather than their abilities to enact
social change or speak out against societal ills. For example, when Ricky Martin
attempted to speak from political spaces, particularly against the injustice of
bombings in Vieques, he was trivialized because he had already been framed
within a highly sexual and restrictive Latin lover script (Calafell *More Than
a Latin Lover*). The Latina/o public intellectual/entertainer was largely nonexistent or unrecognizable … that is, until El Vez. Though El Vez had been
performing for years before the Latin Explosion/Invasion, I argue that it was not
until his appearance in the documentaries *Americanos: Latino Life in the United
States* and *El Rey De Rock 'N Roll* that he reached mass audiences.[1]

He has been called many things, including the Mexican Elvis (Blackwell), MEXKING (Gonzalez "All That Glitters"), transculturator of popular culture (Habell-Pallán "El Vez Is"), and the hardest working Chicano in the music business (Gonzalez "All That Glitters"). El Vez was born in 1988 when Robert Lopez, the curator of La Luz de Jesús Gallery in California, became inspired by Elvis folk art and an affinity he perceived between Chicanas/os and Elvis Presley (Gonzalez "All That Glitters"). To locate this affinity, Lopez did not have to look too far from home. As a boy, he had always thought Elvis Presley was Mexican: "They (Mexicans) invented the velvet painting of Elvis and made many busts of him" ("El Vez Happening"). Lopez elaborates, "When I was a kid I thought Elvis was Chicano. With his dark slicked-back hair, he looked just like one of my uncles" (Gonzalez); "I had uncles with continental slacks and slight pompadours in that Elvis style" ("El Vez Happening").

Inspired by a combination of reverence, affinity, and irreverence, Lopez debuted El Vez at Weep Weak, the annual celebration of Elvis' birthday in Memphis. Keeping in mind folk musician Phil Ochs' statement "If there's hope for America, it's in a revolution. If there's any hope for a revolution, it lies in Elvis Presley becoming Che Guevara" (Gonzalez "All That Glitters"), El Vez infuses Chicana/o history and ideologies into the popular culture of the mainstream audiences through the lens of Elvis Presley. Carolina Gonzalez, a writer for *Frontera Magazine*, paraphrases El Vez, who sees himself as "an entertainer first, but with a subversive intent," as someone who "wants to reflect on 'what it takes to get people interested in the revolution,' while questioning the extent to which the revolutionary ideal is romanticized into guerrilla chic" ("All That Glitters"). El Vez has produced several albums over the course of the past decade; some of his better-known compact discs include *Graciasland*, *Son of a Lad From Spain*, and more recently *Boxing with God*

Theorist Michelle Habell-Pallán argues that "El Vez's performance also calls into question traditional definitions of nationhood, masculinity, and the criteria by which human rights and citizenship are granted to or withheld from subjects of the nation" ("El Vez Is" 198). In general, scholars, including Habell-Pallán and Jose David Saldívar, have celebrated El Vez's project of superimposing Chicana/o cultural histories and nuances onto the Elvis Presley persona, or telling "the story of Latino history through the music of Elvis Presley" (Miserandino). Though I recognize and value the subversive and empowering aspects of El Vez's performances, I also want to complicate things by raising questions rather than offering answers.

I must admit I situate myself in a space of ambivalence. I am very much in support of El Vez's project, even to the point of perhaps calling myself a fan, yet simultaneously there has always been a critical part of me that is not quite ready to give my support unconditionally. It has been difficult for me to name my hesitation, and I am reluctant to admit this publicly. Perhaps it is my inability to get past the sign of Elvis Presley. Perhaps it is how I cringe when I hear the rhetoric of the American Dream. This has been my uncertainty for years in writing this piece. Thus, in this essay I explore some of the spaces of what I consider to be contradiction in Lopez's/El Vez's performance.

For several years I have used El Vez/Robert Lopez as a point of discussion about Chicana/o identities in the courses I teach on issues of race, ethnicity, and rhetoric. Each semester the students' responses range from uncritical celebration to outright contempt. All too often students of color chastise Lopez for presenting his message through a "white sign" (Elvis), arguing that his reappropriation is not enough, that whiteness is still privileged. I challenge them to consider what are the politics of El Vez reappropriating a potentially oppressive sign (Presley) that was in fact viewed as oppressive because of Presley's own tactics of appropriation? Is something being done in that? What can we say about power in this situation? The class is often not convinced or impressed. After viewing the documentary *El Rey de Rock 'N Roll*, two Chicanas from California vehemently criticized Lopez/El Vez, questioning Lopez's authenticity to tell the stories he tells when he performs as El Vez. They wondered aloud how a punk rock kid can embody the story of a *cholo* in the barrio. They argued he was embodying Conquergood's critique of the infatuation of the enthusiast who enters with an anthropological gaze of superficiality. Is there a sense of privilege in being able to perform and walk away from that socially maligned identity, while others cannot? Other students have questioned the audience for whom El Vez was performing, arguing he was embodying modern-day minstrelsy. Some students have felt he is a misogynist. Overwhelmingly, every semester students question whether the progressive and political lyrics that El Vez sings are enough. What if the audience cannot critically interpret or unpack the embodiment? I remind the students of El Vez's pointed commentary between his songs and his manipulation of popular culture and visuals to make critiques. He certainly did these things each time I saw him perform live. The students' critiques caused me to be more aware of my own uncritical embracement of Lopez/El Vez and necessitated this work. Does the fact that the students are not seeing El Vez in the actual state of performance, but simply through reproductions on video tape and compact disc, affect their reading?

Are they missing the affective political charge of El Vez and his music? Though I do not intend to gauge audience reception, I do take the students' critiques seriously and use them to guide many of the questions I explore in this essay. Some of the critiques mirror my own questions and unresolved issues in watching a performer like El Vez.

While I value El Vez's work and find it highly political, all of the questions raised by the students caused me to consider the need to examine how these performances may rearticulate the politics they disavow in the desire to create spaces of coalition and education. Thus, operating from an urge for sustained critique, I critically examine Robert Lopez/El Vez to raise questions about the ways in which he may be both complicit in and challenging to dominant discourses. Loosely working within theories of public and hidden transcripts as described by James Scott, as well as theories of disidentification and excess, I examine Robert Lopez's public performances as El Vez, while his backstage and public performances as the artist/activist Robert Lopez undermine this potential complicity through difference. I use El Vez not simply to add to work examining Chicana/o activism and performance but also to add to theories of resistance and complicity within performative or mediated spaces. The performances of El Vez and Lopez work together to critique dominant systems of power through performances of excess, difference, and disidentification.

Performing Resistance

Scholars within performance studies have long been concerned with the ways historically marginalized people resist the interpellative power of dominant discourse. Writing of the resistive strategies that queers of color use in their creation of a middle space that neither assimilates nor entirely resists dominant ideology, José Esteban Muñoz has offered the process of disidentification. Muñoz writes, "The version of identity politics that this book participates in imagines a reconstructed narrative of identity formation that locates the enacting of self at precisely the point where the discourses of essentialism and constructivism short-circuit" (*Disidentification* 6). This process of working simultaneously on and against dominant ideology often lends itself to performances of excess or excessive stereotype, as in the case of performance artist Carmelita Tropicana. Of performance artists such as Tropicana, Marga Gomez, and Vaginal Crème Davis, Muñoz writes, "Although they participate in the genre of comedy and satire, these performances do not lose sight of the fact that humor is a valuable pedagogical and political project" (*Disidentification* xi). Thus, the excessive or over-the top performances created by each of these performers mirror Lancaster's argument that excess or recognition of the play of excess creates spaces for critique.

In a similar vein, but writing from an anthropological perspective, James Scott discusses public and hidden transcripts and performances for disempowered communities. Scott states, "Subordinates offer a performance of deference and consent while attempting to discern, to read, the real intentions and mood of the potentially threatening powerholder" (3). Of what he terms the public transcript, Scott notes that it "will typically, by its accommodationist tone, provide convincing evidence for the hegemony of dominant values, for the hegemony of dominant discourses" (4). In relation to the public transcript, Scott theorizes the hidden transcript as "discourse that takes place 'offstage,' beyond direct observation by powerholders. The hidden transcript is thus derivative in the sense that it consists of those offstage speeches, gestures, and practices that confirm, contradict, or inflect what appears in the public transcript" (4–5). Scott argues that the hidden transcript is restricted in its performance as it is not a matter of public record. A second vital aspect of the hidden transcript is that it is not simply limited to speech acts but also is embodied or performed. Finally, Scott reminds us that the zone between the hidden and public transcript is a site of constant struggle.

Scott's work on hidden and public transcripts can be likened to Erving Goffman's work on front and backstage behavior. Conceptualizing human behavior through the metaphor of performance, Goffman defines the front as a public performance. Within these performances are settings that Goffman sees as "scenic parts of expressive equipment[;] one may take the term 'personal front' to refer to the other items of expressive equipment, the items that we most intimately identify with the performer himself and that we naturally expect will follow the performer wherever he goes" (23–24). Recognizing how the performance is socialized, molded, or modified to fit the expectations of society, Goffman argues that public or frontstage performances will most often incorporate or exemplify the values of the society. Just as Goffman theorizes a frontstage, he also theorizes a backstage as a place where, "relative to a given performance, ... the impression fostered by the performance is knowingly contradicted as a matter of course" (112). Conceptualizing identity and performance through the public transcript can similarly be likened to some strategies of passing in that there is an element of façade. Writing of what he terms interiorized passing in the work of performance artist Vaginal Crème

Davis, Muñoz notes that passing is not about direct opposition to the dominant paradigm, that in some cases the passer may simultaneously reject and identify with the dominant paradigm (*Disidentification* 108).

From Scott, Muñoz, and Goffman we see the complex realms of identity, performance, and resistance. Loosely working within Scott's theories of hidden and public transcripts, Goffman's approach of identity as performance, and Munoz's theory of disidentification, I attempt to bridge and extend these theories of resistance with performance art–based theories to understand the multilayered performance of Robert Lopez/El Vez. By examining Lopez/El Vez through these lenses I hope to study the spaces between accommodation and resistance and struggle and reproduction. Rather than focusing primarily upon El Vez's lyrics, I choose to focus on the politics surrounding the performance, rhetoric, and embodiment of El Vez, as well as Robert Lopez's own self-presentations in interviews. Playing these images against one another we begin to understand the efficacy of each of the performances. While the political importance of El Vez's lyrics is clearly indisputable, as he is known for remixing Elvis Presley classics with Chicano-laced themes, the discourses espoused by Lopez/El Vez, his audience, and through his performance still merit critical attention. Therefore, while I occasionally draw upon his music, I focus primarily upon interviews, the documentary *El Rey de Rock 'N Roll*, and his segment in *Americanos: Latino Life in the United States*.

I begin with my decision to focus on El Vez and his embodiments rather than solely his lyrics. I follow with a discussion of the "contradictions" of the public performance of El Vez and the ways that Robert Lopez's backstage performances disidentify with the potentially problematic parts of El Vez's performance. I do not attempt to offer any large-scale judgment, but rather raise questions and tease out issues in order to complicate the conversation about El Vez.

Onstage: El Vez/Offstage: Robert Lopez

Although it has been demonstrated that the lyrical content of El Vez's songs offers challenges to dominant discourses that flatten Chicana/o identities (Habell-Pallán "El Vez Is"; *Loca Motion*), critical assessment of El Vez's persona and performance calls for more attention. Through the trope of excess I seek to critically interrogate spaces of complicity and resistance within El Vez's performances. More specifically, I examine his embodiment of the exotic, erotic Other, his use of the rhetoric of the American Dream, his employment of a white cultural icon, and his commodification of identity.

Historically, representations of Latina/os in the United States have been extremely limiting, problematic, and racist. Respective examinations by Keller and Rodriguez (*Heroes, Lovers*) have traced the myriad stereotypes and one-dimensional depictions of Latino sexuality and masculinity. Images have ranged from that of the *bandido* to the greaser or gang member, but perhaps one of the most pervasive images of Latino masculinity has been that of the Latin lover. Historically, the Latin lover has come to represent the exotic, foreign, or sensual Other whose sole desire is sex—and primarily sex with white women. Delgado and Calafell have marked recent shifts in this representation through their examination of pop star Ricky Martin, who imbued the stereotype with a sexual ambiguity that had not previously been present. Thus, because of the prevalence of this script along with the already eroticized images of Elvis "the pelvis" Presley, it comes as no surprise that El Vez would come to embody a sexually charged exotic Other, a well-known script for Latino males in popular culture.

El Vez performs the hyper-heterosexual exotic Other through his sexual dance moves, form-fitting costumes, and suggestive dialogues with members of the audience. Through his constant costume changes, and in particular his use of rip-away clothes, El Vez pulls the attention to his body, a space of pleasure or of consumption. Audience members are invited to gaze upon El Vez's body, causing one woman to say, "He is so hot I could lick him" (*El Rey de Rock n' Roll*). Habell-Pallán argues that "El Vez subverts traditional masculinity by 'opening up his body for objectification and thus signals a collapse of the traditional gendered hierarchy of looking'" (*Loca Motion* 200). Furthermore, after concerts and even in the documentary *El Rey de Rock n' Roll*, we see female admirers vying for a sweat-soaked towel that El Vez uses throughout the performance. In one instance in the documentary, El Vez is shown autographing a towel for a woman, then taking a second to rub it over his chest again in order to give her some more of his mythical mojo (*El Rey*). In another example of El Vez embodying the Latin lover/sexual icon space, a woman is holding El Vez saying that it is her ultimate fantasy to have one ten-minute slow dance with him, while another woman has to be almost forcibly removed from the stage and El Vez's body (*El Rey*). El Vez embodies hyper-heterosexuality and hyper-hegemonic masculinity, which have the potential to critique dominant ideologies. Habell-Pallán argues that El Vez performs "gender drag" through "kinging" (*Loca Motion*).

While these performances offer the possibility for resistive readings, I, like my students, wonder whether all audiences are prepared, willing, and able to make these readings. Are some audiences willing to read him beyond the kitsch factor that is so often desired and consumed? Does the performance move from mimesis (imitation of experience) to poiesis (meaning) to kinesis (intervention)? The question of audience reception could be reminiscent of Delgado's reading of Chicano rapper Kid Frost in that the message of the performer is not necessarily geared to a mass audience; rather, the ideal audience is other Chicana/os who know the slang and situations he describes ("Chicano Ideology Revisited; All Along the Border"). Thus, we may want to ask: Who is the audience for El Vez? This is not to suggest that we essentialize or delimit an audience; rather, perhaps, we should consider the critical lenses and theories of the flesh the audience brings in their decoding of a performance.

Interestingly, Lopez's hidden transcript, which I adapt here from Scott's original context and view instead as a backstage or disidentifactory strategy, elaborates on the constructedness of the El Vez persona. Of the hidden transcript Scott writes, "We cannot know how contrived or imposed the performance is unless we can speak, as it were, to the performer offstage, out of this particular power-laden context, or unless the performer suddenly declares openly on stage, that the performance we have previously observed were just a pose" (4). Discussing El Vez's hyper-heterosexual performance and how he negotiates it with his own identity, Lopez states, "Sexuality is a great thing and has a lot to do with rock and roll. ... I'm gay, but El Vez is straight. I mean he's a character. El Vez isn't me" (*El Rey*). Similarly, discussing El Vez's performances of exaggerated *Chicanismo* or machismo, as he draws upon *cholo* and gang symbolism in his songs such as "In the Barrio" and its accompanying video, Lopez states, "I wasn't in a gang. I didn't have a lowrider car. El Vez is a character. El Vez is a culmination of many facets of my life. Not all facets I've experienced" (*El Rey*). Lopez juxtaposed with the El Vez character offers a view of the multiple possibilities of Chicana/o identities while highlighting the constructedness of images such as the Latin lover.

The consumption of El Vez by audience members is even more complex because El Vez performs within the sexually charged sign of Elvis Presley, whose television performances were often shot from the waist up because of his suggestive dancing. The sign from which he operates is already imbued with a hyper-sexuality that demands this performance. Commentators have noted that many of the spectators at the El Vez shows are perhaps reliving their youth or youthful sexual angst for Presley (*El Rey*). Embodying Elvis,

El Vez adds other sexual politics to the icon through the introduction of themes of safe sex, as in the song "Rubbernecking." While I do not necessarily want to focus on El Vez's lyrics, as Saldívar and Habell-Pallán have already made persuasive arguments about their political efficacy, it is important to note the ways they work to temper a misreading of his hyper-heterosexual performance. As discussed at the start of this essay, when performer Ricky Martin, also filtered through the Latin lover mode and performing in excess of it, attempted to speak outright politically about situations in Vieques he was mocked rather than taken seriously. However, El Vez's playing to the stereotype or dominant scripts or in excess of them open up spaces for possibilities where a comic frame permits him to slyly interject political themes into his message in a way that is campy. For audiences who might not have the cultural capital to read the codes of excess that El Vez employs as a means of critique, the song lyrics and on-stage commentary, juxtaposed with his over-the-top (potentially read by some as stereotypical) representation of Latino masculinity, potentially allow for interpretation and understanding of his underlying politics.

Reflexively speaking about stereotypes and their efficacy, Robert Lopez comments, "I think stereotypes exist and are nothing to be afraid of but they are not everyone in every community. Everybody has their own individual person. I do not represent all Mexican culture past, present, and future. I am one Mexican" (*El Rey*). Interestingly, Lopez comments on the political possibilities of stereotypes, but fails to acknowledge the translation factor within the realm of stereotype. While discourses of whiteness and white identity by default get to occupy multiple spaces or possibilities, the paucity of images of Latina/os creates a situation in which there is very little complexity and each representation matters. Thus, while Lopez recognizes the power of stereotypes, he fails to acknowledge issues regarding the politics of representation and self-definition through a rhetoric of individuality and publicity. Perhaps Lopez seeks a middle space, as identified by Muñoz as a space in which stereotype is employed and remade (*Disidentification*). Or perhaps Lopez, in his embodiment and performance of stereotype, is actually performing a public transcript that is seemingly complicit in dominant ideologies but behind the scenes tells another story. Of the issue of power and its relationship to the public transcript, Scott writes, "The greater disparity in power between dominant and subordinate and the more arbitrarily it is exercised, the more the public transcript will take on a more stereotyped, ritualistic cast. In other words, the more menacing the power, the thicker the mask" (3).

Commenting in unaccented speech about his exaggerated accent and its potential to reinforce stereotypes of Otherness, El Vez states, "If someone wants to call me a stereotype because of my accent, well Latinos have accents sometimes. Some don't. Some blend into white yuppies which is fine too" (*El Rey*). Thus, the image of El Vez embodying signifiers of the exotic Other Latin lover, thick accent, insatiable sexual appetite, and machismo may be a performance of a public transcript that needs to be read alongside a hidden transcript to gauge resistance, or perhaps Lopez performs a complicit stereotype but imbues it with difference by queering or culturally syncretizing the potentially oppressive icon Elvis Presley. Within the process of cultural syncretism, dominant elements are ripped out of context and reconstituted or translated through a different cultural perspective from the original and imbued with vernacular references.

El Vez, through his accent, costumes, dancing, and hyper-heterosexuality, performs as the ideal exotic Other to be gazed upon and consumed, but in the hope that in that consumption, politics will also be consumed. Between 1999 and 2000, a clear trend toward the commodification of all things Latina/o emerged whereby Latina/o cultures became mass-marketed and there was mass production for insatiable public consumption (Cepeda "Columbus Effect(s)"). The most powerful example of this disposable commodity relationship can be observed by looking at the rise and "fall" of pop star Ricky Martin, who never quite reached the same mainstream crossover success as his first English-language album *Ricky Martin*. The consumption of Martin's likeness was everywhere because of his mainstream appeal; in contrast, when examining El Vez, who has emerged as a counterpublic of sorts, his consumption takes place at another level—the level of camp or kitsch that has the ability to make self-reflexive or self-conscious critiques. For example, fans visiting El Vez's website quickly learn that they too can own a lock of hair from the head of the king himself. The consumption of the Other goes as far as buying a lock of hair from El Vez; however, much like the performer himself, the sale is presented in an over-the-top, campy, and self-conscious way. Buyers are encouraged to buy a lock of hair that can be used for multiple purposes, including "for lockets, cloning, Santaria, etc …" all complete in a "deluxe" ziplock bag. All of this for the incredible price of $3.00! Conversely, if owning a piece of the Other is too much, buyers can instead indulge in getting themselves a swatch of fabric from El Vez's stage costume with an authentification card for the low price of $3.00. I must admit I have been a consumer of a lot of this merchandise. I desire this merchandise not because I want to get a bit of the Other but because of the affect of subversion it brings.

Each of these items marks much of the politics of El Vez and his ability to revel in or dwell within the possibilities of contradiction or the ridiculous. Embodying stereotype and playing up commodification and consumerism, El Vez plays each of these roles to the hilt using humor or ridicule as his way out or as a means of critique, similar to strategies discussed by Muñoz (*Disidentification*).

Inevitably, those who question El Vez will point to his adoption of the potentially oppressive symbol of Elvis Presley and his parroting of the ideology and rhetoric of the American Dream. I have already briefly discussed the use of Elvis Presley, but I want to spend more time discussing the pairing of this image with the rhetoric of the American Dream. Outside of his El Vez persona, discussing his ethnic identity, Lopez relates, "I call myself a Chicano" (*Americanos*). Lopez's Chicano education was gained through personal reflection and reading rather than Chicano studies courses. He traces his Chicano consciousness to memories of wanting to rebel against his family's claims that they were from Spain, not Mexico—a tactic used by many Mexican Americans seeking to assimilate into mainstream white culture through a claim of fabled whiteness. El Vez continues to discuss his identity politics by affirming the Aztec image within Chicana/o rhetoric as "high," because "we don't need to use the European image of what is high" (*Americanos*). This is a very common rhetorical strategy used by the Chicano movement (Hammerback, Jensen, and Gutíerrez). Though Lopez makes a conscious effort to align himself and El Vez with a Chicana/o politics, when interviewed he also makes continual references to the American Dream or the Horatio Alger story as the impetus for his work. To locate or align oneself politically with Chicana/o ideology is to accept Chicano as a signifier for solidarity against a history of racial oppression and discrimination at the hands of Anglo-Americans (Gutiérrez 184). The coupling of the American Dream with a Chicana/o consciousness creates a contradiction or a rupture that may underscore the power of El Vez's work. Here Lopez describes some goals of his performances as El Vez:

"Elvis is the king of the American dream," explains Lopez. "I want to show my audience that you don't have to be a white male to make it. It's all done in a show-biz light, but it's serious at the same time. It's about Chicano pride. When people leave an El Vez show, I want them to be happy to be Mexican even if they're not." (Blackwell)

Everyone's different, but you still have to be proud. It's the old idea, people will come and say, "I come to your show and I walk away proud to be Mexican, and I'm not, and I'm white" [which is no small feat in a state that constantly constructs Mexicans as inferior]. It's the idea of instilling pride, and you could fill in the blank.

> I mean I am El Vez, the blank Elvis, black, gay, straight, Asian or whatever. (As qtd.
> in Habell-Pallán 188)

Seeing El Vez as a vehicle for instilling pride in Chicana/os as well as in white Americans, Lopez elaborates on the relationship between the American Dream and popular culture by offering El Vez as the

> king as empowerment ... king as poor man with nothing turning into greatest entertainer of all time (success—working from nothing to top American dream) AMERICAN DREAM ... you don't have to be a white man in your 40s to be part of the American dream ... it's for everyone ... because that is America ... El Vez, the Elvis you could fit in anything ... I super-impose my culture and heritage over American icons ... because that's what America is about. (As qtd. in Miserandino)
>
> I think Americans forget that America is supposed to be about equal opportunity rights for all. (As qtd. in *Americanos*)

Casting Elvis Presley as the king of success stories, Lopez hopes to overlay potential Chicana/o success upon a similar narrative.

To unpack Lopez's statements and his process of overlaying culture, we must begin with the rags-to-riches narrative of Elvis Presley. The most popular narrative of the Elvis Presley success story goes something like this: Elvis was born on January 8, 1935, to Gladys and Vernon Presley "in a two-room house" in Tupelo, Mississippi ("Overview"). His twin brother, Jessie Garon, was stillborn. He moved with his parents to Memphis, Tennessee, in 1948. In 1954, he began his singing career with the Sun Records label in Memphis. A year later his recording contract was sold to RCA Victor, and by 1956 he was an international sensation ("Overview"). In addition to receiving fourteen Grammy nominations, Elvis starred in thirteen films and served in the U.S. Army. He died at his Memphis home, Graceland, on August 16, 1977.

Presley's success story is illustrative of the Horatio Alger story in that a poor man can make good and overcome obstacles such as poverty to assume a place of prominence and success in society. Within an immigrant context, the story asserts that if one works hard enough in a new country, one can succeed financially. Linking Presley with the narrative of the American Dream can be problematic because, regardless of Presley's class origins, he still had the privilege of whiteness that cannot be performed or accessed by all immigrants who get marked as Other because of skin color or language. This same critique is made by Martin and Yep, who criticize the ways that Eminem uses his past economic disadvantages to symbolically claim oppression and deny the ways he benefits from white privilege. Not all immigrants can achieve the material benefits of whiteness, because not all can pass or choose to pass. Furthermore, the rhetoric of the American Dream becomes even more problematic when located within the realm of theories of Chicana/o identities, because to ascribe to this identity is to place oneself on the borderlands as being neither Mexican nor U.S. American, rather as existing in (an)other space. The American Dream is antithetical to a Chicana/o politic because of its uncritical, unconditional assimilationist tendencies. Cultural critic José David Saldívar accounts for El Vez's referencing of the American Dream narrative by writing:

> Rather than vilify the shared dilemmas of other ethno-racial groups whose icons and narratives have transformed U.S. immigrant writing into national archetypes, El Vez aligns the plight of undocumented Mexican workers with those archetypes and symbologies that scholars such as Werner Sollors and Thomas J. Ferraro have shown to be part and parcel of the national imagery: WASPs, after all, in Ferraro's words, "fled religious prosecution," and ethno-racial minorities "were forcibly removed, incorporated, enslaved, and interned." (194)

Saldívar argues that El Vez appropriates the tropes of immigration writings to offer a counter-narrative or what I term a poached narrative that must conform to master discourses. Michelle Habell-Pallán argues that "El Vez's performance visually and viscerally demonstrates that Chicano history *is* American history and vice versa. Hence, many of El Vez's lyrics … narrativize why immigrant and non-immigrant populations in the U.S. who are racialized as non-white should be recognized as part of American national culture" ("El Vez Is" 198). She adds that

> by positing a "family of resemblance" that links the history of many Chicanos—a working-class past and/or present—to Elvis' own childhood of poverty, El Vez's performance connects Mexican American working-class histories to those of most other Americans and highlights the fact that any notion of multiculturalism is incomplete without understanding how class and racial position makes some residents of the United States more equal than others. (*Loca Motion* 188)

Habell-Pallán asserts that El Vez operates in a non-essentialist mode that disrupts any static discourse about identity and instead favors a borderlands or hybrid identity ("El Vez").

In *The Practice of Everyday Life*, Michel de Certeau writes of the ways in which those who are disempowered in society "make do" or invent products tactically. De Certeau begins by deconstructing the concept of consumption, asking what consumers do and make of images they receive (31). Consumption, de

Certeau writes, is "characterized by its ruses, its fragmentation (the result of the circumstances), its poaching, its clandestine nature, its tireless but quiet activity, in short its quasi-invisibility, since it shows itself not in its own products (where will it place them?) but in the art of using those imposed on it" (31). What is important within the process of cultural poaching is that this imposed knowledge becomes used in new ways by consumers that reflect different interests and desires (32–34). This activity of making do consists of selecting fragments from various sources to create new stories or possibilities (35). De Certeau notes, "What is counted is *what* is used, not the *ways* of using" (35). Making do or the process of poaching "produces the ideology of consumption-as-a-receptacle. ... By challenging 'consumption' as it is conceived and (of course) confirmed by these 'authorial' enterprises, we may be able to discover creative activity where it has been denied that any exists, and to relativize the exorbitant claim that *a certain kind* of production (real enough, but not the only kind) can set out to produce history by 'informing' the whole of a country" (166).

Of this process of poaching and its subversive possibilities, de Certeau notes that in creating texts the reader fragments are removed from their spaces of intention and combined in ways that create multiple possibilities or meanings (169). Similar to the postmodern practice of pastiche, "it becomes a text only in its relation to the exteriority of the reader, by an interplay of implications and ruses between two sorts of 'expectation' in combination" (170). Within the process, "the operation of encoding, which is articulated on signifiers, produces the meaning, which is thus not defined by something deposited in the text, by an 'intention,' or by an activity on the part of the author" (171). As noted by de Certeau, the text "becomes a cultural weapon, a private hunting reserve" (171).

One could certainly view Lopez's overlaying of *Chicanismo* on the Elvis Presley persona as cultural poaching and resistive or as the way oppressive ideologies are disidentified within the public transcript. For example, in discussing his use of the United Farm Workers Flag in his performance, El Vez argues that it is very Third Reichian and that "I use it to show one of the ideas of the oppressed people using the worst symbols of the oppressor" (*El Rey*). However, the tension between accommodation and stereotype and resistance remains. Lopez's public transcript is complicit in that it parrots dominant ideologies in his El Vez interview persona as well as in the tension between stereotype and excess through possible disidentification. Thus, perhaps El Vez's use of the American Dream mythology is employed critically as a commentary that does not necessarily seek to alter the ideology, but instead calls attention to its impossibilities.

Furthermore, through narratives of hardship, while seeking to embrace the ideology of the American Dream by discursively placing himself as an outsider to the ideology, El Vez offers a critique from a distance that still allows him to perform in seemingly accommodationist or assimilationist tones that do not isolate or alienate potential white audiences/allies. El Vez offers a cursory reaction to the contested ideology of the American Dream through his music and lyrics. El Vez speaks more specifically through a Chicana/o perspective, recognizing how racism and discrimination get played out in larger structures such as the system of immigration in the United States. One such case is his song "Immigration Time," in which he complicates traditional Ellis Island narratives by inserting a narrative of border crossing.

What is to be made of Lopez's embodiment or poaching of the Elvis persona, which is then infused with "progressive" politics and contextualized against the backdrop of the American Dream? Saldívar and Habell-Pallán tend to favor the idea that El Vez is reconfiguring a static movement rhetoric into a more inclusive or hybrid space: "El Vez does not equate social constructions of racial and class difference with inferiority or superiority. Instead, he suggests that one can be proud of difference, that one should not suppress it, and that one should not have to pay the consequences for being different" (Habell-Pallán "El Vez Is" 199). They argue that this reconfiguration takes place on several levels, including the reconfiguration of Aztlán, the Chicano homeland, used as a symbol of empowerment and unity during the Chicano movement. Historian David Gutiérrez, writing of the use of Aztlán during the Chicano movement, notes, "The young activists presented a quasi-nationalist vision of the Chicano people which extolled a pre-Columbian, native ancestry while diminishing or even rejecting their connection with American culture and society" (185). This disavowal of "American" culture would include a rejection of assimilation "as nothing more than *gabacho* attempts to maintain hegemony over Chicanos by destroying their culture" (185). Rhetorician Fernando Delgado argues that Aztlán served as a central ideograph during the Chicano movement. Ideographs are links between rhetoric and ideology, words with culturally nuanced understanding, and have a constitutive element (McGee). Thus, in reconfiguring Aztlán there is the possibility of relinquishing some of its constitutive potential. Of El Vez's reconfiguration of Aztlán, Saldívar offers,

If Aztlán as a metaphor for identity based on originary claims on land needs ... to be replaced by other paradigms, El Vez desires to hold on to some of Aztlán viability as a symbol. ... Aztlán becomes in the song a heterotopic space where documented and undocumented subjects can exist. ... As a signifier for cultural dispossession and

> imaginary reconstruction, "Aztlán" suggests a rather different "autotopia" than we've seen, for the song does not celebrate protonationalist Chicano movement wholeness but makes room for heterogeneous fragmentariness. … he contests the traditional pathological view of diaspora and border-crossing experiences. (195)

As the Latina/o population continues to grow in numbers in the United States as well as to disperse throughout the nation, the question of the usefulness of Aztlán as a point of identification becomes important. Will Aztlán be necessary for a political project (Calafell "Disrupting the Dichotomy")? Does El Vez recognize this and thus offer a reconstructed Aztlán? Though El Vez is unique in his cultural poaching of the Elvis persona as well as his rewriting of songs by David Bowie, Rod Stewart, and Iggy Pop, he is not unique in his attempts to refashion Chicana/o, as others such as Moraga (*The Last Generation*) and performance artist Luis Alfaro have attempted to queer Aztlán.

Conclusions/Thoughts

Through my discussion of El Vez/Lopez it has become clear that reading the public/frontstage performance alongside his hidden/backstage persona creates multiple possibilities out of such a complex performer and performance. While I do not imagine that the discourses Lopez espouses are in any way hidden, I am interested in how they are shadowed by the larger-than-life excesses of El Vez. However, when these backstage performances are read alongside El Vez, do the politics of these multiple layered performances come to the surface? Much of this analysis is preliminary, seeking to build upon work conducted by previous scholars and raise new questions. Overall, I find Lopez/El Vez to be progressive in his use of excess and offstage performance as a means of critique. El Vez plays excessively and almost over the top to the stereotype, while Lopez further tempers and reveals their constructedness. El Vez embraces commodification then undermines it through ridicule. Each of these strategies leads me to see El Vez/Lopez as performing in critically oriented ways that are undermining and challenging system of power through excess.

I call myself an ambivalent fan. I will continue to support El Vez. I will continue to use him in my classes. I will wear my "El Vez for Prez" T-shirt as I walk across campus listening to *Graciasland* on my iPod, but I will never completely give up my "suspicious mind."

· 5 ·

TO RICKY WITH LOVE

This is my culture, my entertainment, nothing to laugh over, this is me.

(Serros 30)

At the school from which I received my MA, I will forever be known as the graduate student who wrote a thesis on Ricky Martin. This has provided a generally mixed reaction, ranging from the not-too-happy look on the then-director of the program's face when I announced to a group of minority students that they should consider coming to the department because "You too can write a thesis on Ricky Martin!" to being told that Ricky was simply "tabloid scholarship" and not a worthy object of study for Latina/o studies. Though I have only detailed the negative, there has also been a great deal of pleasure in my relationship with Ricky, which is why I continue to come back to him even when it seems as if we have nothing left to say to one another.

In this chapter I work through Ricky Martin's performances of ambiguity, both racial and sexual, to understand how he creates spaces of possibility and at times resistance. I begin with a discussion of Martin's racial and sexual ambiguity and his functioning as a bridge (sometimes contested) between multiple communities. Following this discussion, I elaborate upon the media's construction of Martin's sexual ambiguity and his negotiation of it through disidentification with stereotypes, which remakes ambiguity into a site of resistance. In support of these claims I walk through theories of dance, resistance, *mestizaje,* and passing. I read popular press clippings and analyze television shows (*Ricky Martin: For One Night Only, The 1999 Billboard Music Awards*, and *The 2000 Grammy Awards*) and videos produced during the "Latin Explosion" (1999–2000) through these theories.

Ricky Martin's Body As Text

> Not since Elvis have a pair of hips caused so much excitement.
> (Barbara Walters' 10 Most Fascinating People)

Reduced to his hips. Reduced to his body. Ricky Martin became a focal point in America's popular carnal culture because of his high profile during the "Latin Explosion/Invasion/crossover" of 1999–2000. Though Martin had been an international sensation through his performances in the group Menudo and during his solo career and his acting career in popular Mexican and American soap operas, the Latin Explosion marked his entry into the echelons of U.S. popular culture. Scholars have noted the ways this constructed Othered Latina/os, as if they were somehow outside U.S. popular culture and citizenship (Calafell *More Than*; Cepeda "*Mucho Loco*"; "Columbus Effects"), while also erasing a prior history of Latina/o performers in the United States by implying the newness of Latina/o performers (Cepeda "*Mucho Loco*"; "Columbus Effects"). In looking at Martin it is essential to understand his embodiments of Otherness. The importance of the "minority" celebrity's body as text has been acknowledged as a key site of struggle (Beltrán; Negrón-Muntaner). Martin's body becomes a site of interpretation of Puerto Ricanness, *latinidad*, and Otherness. Visual representations and manipulations of it such as changes in hair color, choices in dress, and body movements become important (Shugart). Each of these "small" aspects of Martin's body has huge implications. For example, of hair Turner writes, "Unlike skin, hair continually grows outwards, erupting from the body into the social space beyond it … hair offers itself as a symbol of the libidinal energies of the self and of the never-ending struggle to constrain within acceptable forms their eruption into social space" (18). Given the importance of Martin's body to popular understandings of *latinidad* or Latina/o identities, I "read" Ricky Martin's body as a text by examining the changes in his appearances just before and during his "crossover" English album *Ricky Martin*. In addition, I examine the ways Martin manipulates his body in performance, skillfully using his body to work in and out of ideology, to resist interpellation, and to enact performative survival strategies of disidentification.

In examining Martin's body as text, it is pertinent to revisit literature regarding passing, more specifically racial passing, as well as literature that addresses the ways that the body communicates through movement and dance. Passing is relevant because Martin must enact certain acceptable "Hispanic" scripts in order to "pass" or "cross over" into the mainstream. This passing manifests itself in his appearance as well as in his movements and dance. Passing is a phenomenon in which marginalized persons take on the "appearance" or persona of the dominator to go into that world—a world previously unavailable to them (Moon). In passing, the person manipulates the body through movement, gesture, voice, and appearance in order to communicate an/other identity.

Of passing, Elaine K. Ginsberg writes, "By extension, 'passing' has been applied discursively to disguises of other elements of an individual's presumed 'natural' or 'essential' identity, including class, ethnicity, and sexuality, as well as gender, the latter usually effected by deliberate alternations of physical appearance and behavior, including cross-dressing" (3). In this alternation of the body there is power in that people are able to access structures of power previously out of their reach. Ginsberg elaborates by noting that within the semantics of the word is the sense that "an individual crossed or passed through a racial line or boundary—indeed trespassed—to assume a new identity, escaping the subordination and oppression accompanying one identity and accessing the privileges and status of the other" (3). Ginsberg is quick to note that passing can be a way to transgress both legal and cultural boundaries (1). Hasian and Nakayama write of the ways in which bodies are legally constructed through their examination of the Susie Phipps court case. Phipps was a "white" woman who discovered that legally she was classified as African American. Upon discovering this fact she went to court to change her racial status, but lost. This case speaks volumes about the ways in which the government controls and regulates bodies. Governments determine and maintain strict racial binaries. Similar to the ways that bodies are sexed, societies carefully distinguish racial bodies (Guillaumin 43).

Inherent in passing is the notion of privilege. When speaking of accessing privilege, specifically of passing by African Americans, Piper writes, "There is the vicarious enjoyment of watching one of our own infiltrate and achieve in a context largely defined by institutionalized attempts to exclude blacks from it" (227). Passing becomes a source of power in that the minority subject can access fluid identities and move beyond socially constructed roles. Both Piper and Ginsberg note that passing can be both liberatory and threatening. Passing can be viewed as threatening to those in the dominant group who have socially constructed boundaries around privileged bodies, and liberatory by those in the oppressed group because it reinscribes socially constructed boundaries and bodies. Ginsberg writes that passing becomes a means of agency for minority subjects by the deconstruction of essentialist norms. She states,

> In its interrogation of the essentialism that is the foundation of identity politics, passing has the potential to create a space for creative self determination and agency; the opportunity to construct new identities, to experiment with multiple subject positions, and to cross social and economic boundaries that exclude or oppress. (16)

Anti-essentialism and the ambiguity of the body make passing possible. Because of histories of colonialism and the slave trade, the Latina/o body has come to represent in many ways an ambiguous or multiracial body. Ambiguity or the defiance of the black/white binary has become a prominent theme in Latina/o autobiographical literature, including writings by Julia Alvarez, Kevin Johnson, and Cherríe Moraga.

I do not argue that Martin literally passes as white; rather, I am interested in the ways he is privy to whiteness and Otherness simultaneously. It could be argued that it was because Martin was white that he was at the forefront of the Latin Explosion. Negrón-Muntaner likens him to Elvis Presley in that he can take the credit for "breaking" Latin music into the mainstream. Martin's whiteness carried the privilege of visibility, enabling him to pass from the terrain of Latina/o Otherness into the public space of whiteness and imbuing it with difference. In addition, Shugart writing of Ellen DeGeneres' heterosexual passing, argues that even as DeGeneres came out she continued to position herself both in and out of heterosexuality. In a similar manner I see Martin as being privy to both discourses of whiteness and *latinidad*. Operating on the level of nationalism, Cepeda sees Shakira as the idealized transitional citizen who can be simultaneously Latina American and U.S. Latina ("Shakira As").

Similar to passing is the strategy of disidentification in which the manipulation and ornamentation of the body becomes central for the minority subject (Muñoz *Disidentification*). The performative body becomes a vehicle for survival. Within this discussion of manipulation and ornamentation it is extremely relevant to consider the role of dance, particularly for someone, like Martin, whose body is a body in motion. Desmond notes that much attention has been placed on the body as text, but rarely has dance been included in this examination (33). She argues that social identities are "signaled, formed, and negotiated through bodily movement" (Desmond 33). Of bodies in motion Celeste Fraser Delgado and José Esteban Muñoz write,

> Dance sets politics in motion, bring together in rhythmic affinity where identification takes the form of histories written on the body through gestures. The body dancing to Latin rhythms analyzes and articulates the conflicts that have crossed Latin/o American identity and history from the conquest of the continent to California's passage of the racist Proposition 187. (10)

Latin dance offers counterhistories. It is resistive in its reclamation of subjugated histories (Delgado and Muñoz 16–17). Delgado and Muñoz note that "Latin/o bodies serve as the site of a long history of racial, cultural, and economic conflict" and that in dance these histories are reinscribed and reinterpreted (10). Desmond, questioning the parameters of "acceptable" movement in American society, asks, "Why are some dances, some ways of moving the body, considered forbidden for members of certain social classes, 'races,' sexes?" (35). Desmond elaborates by explaining that ethnic and cultural dance becomes "toned-down," "tamed," or "whitened" for the non-Latina/o American public's consumption. Writing specifically of Latin dance and American consumption of it, Desmond notes that dance becomes a sanctioned way of expressing sexuality, "especially sexuality associated with subtle, sensuous rotation of the pelvis" (48). Similarly, Richard Dyer argues of Euro-Americans' use of tanning, "In becoming darker, white people may wish to take on some of the imputed characteristics of dark people, characteristics themselves related to the associations of such people in some discourses with healthiness and leisure … dark people are somehow more natural, dark people have the sensuality and fun sought in leisure" (*White* 49). The sensuality of Others is "safely" accessed through dance and appearance. Of Latin dance Píedra notes that "Others" preserve their hidden or protected identities through exaggerated movements. Furthermore, of movement, Young writes, "Postures and gestures are perceived and experienced as manifestations or representations of states of mind. … Movement is a corporeal way of knowing. It is loaded with significance" (5, 11).

It is of central importance to examine Martin in relation to the literature regarding passing and dance because they are key concepts in understanding his performances of resistance and ambiguity. His use of exaggerated movements and his ambiguous chameleon appearance serve as strategies of survival and resistance. In referencing Martin as a chameleon, I allude to the ways in which his body is simultaneously white and Other—a position that defies hegemonic racial notions in the United States. How does Martin use his body through alteration of appearance and the use of dance to enact survival strategies? Does he serve as a bridge between white American and Latina/o communities?

Bridging Communities: Ricky Martin's Body Politics

In the title of the landmark anthology *This Bridge Called My Back: Writings by Radical Women of Color*, Gloria Anzaldúa and Cherríe Moraga directly address the ways in which the bodies of people of color often serve as metaphoric bridges between communities. Of this bridge role Anzaldúa writes, "Being a bridge means being a mediator between yourself and your community and white people" ("Bridge, Drawbridge, Sandbar" 223). These communities range from feminist communities to alliances between communities of color and white communities. This notion of the body as a bridge is also discussed by Ono, who writes of his biracial identity as a bridge (120). As demonstrated through the literature on passing and whiteness, the minority body becomes a site of negotiation, negation, or connection with those communities in power. Of whiteness as commodity Dyer writes, "Being visible as white is a passport to privilege; in colonial contexts" (*White* 44).

Understanding Martin's body as a site of struggle, I use the "bridge" metaphor to consider how Martin's body serves as a bridge for white Americans to access "safe" Others' sexuality, similar to hooks' idea of "eating the Other." In addition, Martin's body serves as a racial and sexual bridge between white Americans and Latina/os. As the bridge to the *mestizo* world, he is both everything and nothing—white while simultaneously Other, the product of *mestizaje*, a logic that defies dominant conceptions about race in the United States. Martin's body and his performed Otherness are visual reminders of colonialism. Writing of hybridity in the process of disidentification, Muñoz notes the position of the postcolonial subject: "The post colonial hybrid is a subject whose identity practices are structured around an ambivalent relationship to the signs of the empire and the signs of the 'native'" (*Disidentification* 78). Muñoz continues,

> The hybrid—and terms that can be roughly theorized as equivalents, such Creole or the *mestizo*—are paradigms that can help account for the complexities and impossibilities of identity, but, except for a certain degree of dependence on institutional frames, what a subject can do from her or his position of hybridity is basically open-ended. The important point is that identity practices such as queerness and hybridity are not a priori sites of contestation, but instead, spaces of productivity where identity's fragmentary nature is accepted and negotiated. (Muñoz *Disidentification* 79)

In this capacity of hybrid, Martin negotiates the role of bridge between communities. This fluidity and its embodiment give Martin the privilege of being a chameleon who serves as a point of identification for both Anglo-Americans and Latina/os. Perhaps Martin recognizes his position as a bridge when he says, "Whatever it is that I have to do to unite Puerto Rico or Latin America with the rest of the world, well, let's go for it" (Cagle "The Entertainers").

A Racial Bridge

The Latina/o body manifests *mestizaje* in a constant fight or negotiation with history and colonialism. The body negotiates historical trauma and systematic violence (Muñoz 161). However, scholars have demonstrated the ways in which Latina/o difference is glossed over and generically coded as brown in U.S. popular culture. Arlene Dávila, author of *Latinos Inc.*, notes the predominance of the generic "Latin look": long dark hair and olive skin that is not too dark, but not so white. Difference must be identifiable. The whiteness and blackness in Latina/o communities disappears into a larger black and white dichotomy that denies their existence (Valdivia "Latinas as Radical Hybrid"). Writing about race in Latin American, Raquel Rivera argues that racial categories depend more on color and other physical characteristics, which are also associated with class and ancestry (33). She argues, "In Latin American, skin tone, facial characteristics, hair type, along with class markings such as dress, body language, and speech patterns all have bearing on race. ... Another great difference between the two systems of racial classification is the white-black dichotomy in the United States, which contrasts with the recognition of a wide variety of intermediate racial possibilities in Latin America" (33). The monolithic of brown becomes the dominant frame through which Latina/os are viewed. In examining the ways Martin's body becomes a racial bridge I offer the following quotes:

> His voice isn't great. But he's got the looks, he's got the energy, and he's got backing. ... And he's not too Latin. (Pellegrini "America Goes *Mucho Loco*")
>
> Like a blond-highlighted cross between Tom Cruise and Montgomery Clift. (Essex)

Noting that Martin is not "too Latin" and referencing him with well-known symbols of white masculinity whose sexual orientation has been called into question, Martin becomes a point of reference to whiteness. In his physical appearance Martin manifests whiteness, not only through his skin color but also through his hair, despite the criticism that has been leveled against him for lightening it. One writer notes that Martin has established his Latino credentials (he is from Puerto Rico, speaks Spanish, and was in the supergroup Menudo), but "He is a U.S. citizen, speaks English, acted in the soap opera *General Hospital* and dyes his hair blond" (Watrous "Latin Musicians Discover New Worlds to Conquer"). The writer continues to question Martin's authenticity by again referencing his appearance through a comparison with one of his contemporaries, Elvis Crespo, "The Spanglish version of the song 'Pintame' comes out in a week—and he has not dyed his hair blond, though an English language album is probably inevitable" (Watrous "Latin Musicians Discover New Worlds").

The question of authenticity is also raised by Catalina Rios, who states, "The media is not ready for the diversity of shapes, sizes and shades that make up the Latino community. … Mainstream can't see our authentic selves and doesn't want to know our authentic selves" (as qtd. in Hernandez). The idea that an authentic physical self or phenotype exists is prevalent for those Latina/os who see this as a means of challenging the preference for whiteness through strategic essentialism. I do not devalue the need for non-white or light-skinned images of Latina/os; however, I am hesitant to agree to a politics of essentialism that calls for us to embrace our "authentic selves" by once again moving away from the politics of mixed-raced identities.

Arteaga sheds light on Martin's embodiments of *mestizaje*: "Ambiguity is most significant not so much in the either/or racial binarism, that is, in not quite being either, as in the profound ambiguity of being both" (10–11). It is this ambiguity that Martin uses as his bridging device—the device that will connect interethnic Latina/o communities as well as white American communities. In refusing to fall prey to a strategic essentialism of identity or fall within the monolith of brownness, a strategy used in social movements such as the Chicano movement (Hammerback, Jensen, and Gutíerrez), Martin disidentifies, using his body to challenge both of these texts.

As a result of Martin's disidentification with dominant scripts, two camps emerge: those who see Martin as assimilating through the enactment of physical manifestations of whiteness and those who see him as the embodiment of *mestizaje*—challenging dominant U.S. conceptions of Latina/o identity by being simultaneously white and Other. White or light-skinned Latina/os are common on any Spanish-language television station in the United States, as we have internalized the racist colonial hierarchies, yet in the racist pathology that exists in U.S.-based popular culture, Latinas/o become foreign and Othered (Flores and Hasian). These images of Otherness come to represent "authentic" Latina/o identities (Dávila). Through his appearance, Martin denies that essentialized Otherness by using his body to serve as a profound manifestation of the situation of many Latina/os in the United States—being simultaneously U.S. born and Latina/o culturally, and also European and indigenous and African. The possibilities of *mestizaje* are endless, and Martin's embodiment of *mestizaje* demonstrates these possibilities. However, it is important to recognize, as Negrón-Muntaner has noted, that Martin's whiteness has the potential to once again silence African heritages in Latina/o communities and hybridity is not a universally celebrated concept (Valdivia).

Embracing *mestizaje*, and specifically whiteness, as a cloak of ambiguity is also evidenced in his name. Ricky Martin is an Anglicized derivation of his given name, Enrique Martin Morales; assuming the name Ricky Martin allows him discursive ambiguity. The name "Ricky Martin," as an Anglo version of his given name, allows even his name to serve as a bridge. Negrón-Muntaner further sees the name change as being tied to Martin's desire to distance himself from macho Puerto Rican culture as manifested in Enrique Sr. Instead, Martin desires "a softer, more caring masculinity, sensitive to the mother's vulnerability as a woman" (Negrón-Muntaner 250).

Martin's ethnic ambiguity has been discussed openly by Latina/os. In the article "Is Ricky Martin Really a Puerto Rican (Latino) Phenomenon?" the following quote by Alberto Memmi frames the piece: "The same way many people avoid being seen with their poor relatives, the colonized, sick of assimilation hides his past, his traditions, his roots, in fact they have become dishonored" (Rodriguez-Dominguez). The writer acknowledges Martin's ambiguity, as well as his own feelings:

> I feel the same ambiguity about this musical "Crossover Dream" which is not new, although the press seems to think so … Ricky Martin retains his "Latino" some will say Hispanic flavor because the category was created to make a homogeneous mass of Chicanos, Mexicanos, Boricuas, Guanacos, Cubanos. […] It's easier to sell stuff to us if we lose our distinctiveness. (sic) (Rodriguez-Dominguez "Is Ricky Martin")

Rodriguez-Dominguez criticizes Martin for singing in English and falling prey to the idea that if you "soften the African-Puerto Rican rhythm you will be liked more" ("Is Ricky Martin"). Continuing the criticism, the writer pinpoints Martin's strategy of disidentification or passing, moreover, by offering, "we will have to play 'the game' and engage in mimicry" ("Is Ricky Martin"). Others defend Martin's ambiguity and disidentification by claiming that his music is working in new formats and that his authenticity is unfairly criticized given that white artists who venture to other cultures for inspiration are labeled as experimental (Rodriguez "Ricky's Only One"). Either way the ambiguity surrounding Martin's music and ethnic embodiment do remain contested sites in Latina/o communities. Martin's "neutrality" or working against and within ideology simultaneously is never really neutral, as all his actions are assigned political motives. Perhaps Martin's ambiguity is so disturbing to Latina/o critics because it forces us to recognize the many ambiguities in ourselves. There are no *true* racial essences upon which to base our identities, and Ricky Martin reminds us of that.

Another prominent detractor of Martin's chosen display of *mestizaje* is writer Esmerelda Santiago, who raises a concern of many Latina/os. Santiago feels the current crop of Latina/o singers "could use some skin-tone diversity. She feels the artists who are being promoted to superstardom mostly look Anglo, leaving the darker performers behind" (Farley 78). Santiago says, "It's fascinating to me, and a little upsetting, that this is still the face of the Caribbean. ... I'm sure that there are equally talented and gifted artists out there whose facial features don't conform as much as to the European ideal" (Farley 78). Santiago references Martin's body as a contested site, alluding to his "safeness" for European Americans in that he personifies the (white) fraternity boy. This image is played up in the media, as one writer describes Martin in the following way, alluding to both his whiteness and to his Otherness: "For a Latino pop sensation, Ricky Martin looks a lot like a preppie Ralph Lauren model" (Pellegrini "America Goes *Mucho Loco*"). Martin's appeal lies in his potential for identification across communities.

This theme of universality or "everyman" can be likened to Kenneth Burke's notion of identification, because Latina/os and the Latina/o body are everything yet simultaneously Other. Burke describes identification that occurs when "two people may be identified in terms of some principle they share in common, an 'identification' that does not deny their distinction" (21). Within Martin's embodiment, identification occurs where Latina/os are positioned as uniquely different from other Americans, specifically white Americans, yet at the same time they are positioned as being not that different after all—Martin's body becomes the point of connection manifesting this. A strategy similar to this is also used in the coffee table book *Americanos: Latino Life in the United States*, in which Otherness is rendered palatable (Calafell and Delgado). The site of identification becomes the site of tensions between the assimilation and the recognition of uniqueness. The celebration of differences, but also the recognition of the commonality in those differences, allows Martin to act as a chameleon (a privilege permitted solely because of his whiteness). The chameleon or everyman mentality is echoed by Colombian singer Shakira: "Latino people have a golden key in their hands, a common treasure. The treasure is fusion. The fusion of rhythms, the fusion of ideas. We Latinos are a race of fusion, and that is the music we make. And so at the dawn of a new millennium when everything is said and done, what could possibly happen besides a fusion?" (as qtd. in Farley 76). Martin comes to embody the ambiguity that is needed for one to pass or crossover. This discursive crossover is enabled by a white/Other body—a contradiction in the eyes of many Americans.

Interestingly, Martin alludes to the tensions of the minority body and the ways in which the body is positioned when he discusses his desire to break from stereotypes. He says, "It's all about breaking stereotypes. For me, the fact that people think Puerto Rico is Scarface, that we ride donkeys to school—that has to change" (as qtd. in Essex). By naming what he sees himself in opposition to, Martin positions not only what he is not but also what he refuses to enact.

A Bridge to "Other" Sexuality

One way in which Martin remains "dark" is in the white American imagination of foreign sexuality. hooks writes of this phenomenon as eating or getting a bit of the Other. Simply put, this is the idea that there "is pleasure to be found in the acknowledgement and enjoyment of racial difference. … ethnicity becomes spice, seasoning that can liven up the dull dish that is mainstream white culture" (21). This idea certainly holds currency with Martin, whose appeal was largely based on his dancing abilities, his shaking his "bon-bon." Both Desmond and Píedra have noted the ways in which Latino dance becomes a safe site for whites to access "Other" or "dark" sexuality; similarly Dyer notes the ways in which whites tan the skin to appear more "natural" or "sensual" (*White*). Martin's music and dance serve as a bridge for white Americans to an Other sexuality. Through the exoticization and sexualization of Martin's body and its movements Other sexuality becomes accessible and safe. Martin's sexuality, movements, and body are reduced to catchphrases. The following examples are representative:

He's a Winston diamond—flawless, perfect (Keogh, as qtd. in "Best and Worst Dressed '99: Ricky Martin" 98).

Classy and manly. … he's so hot, I could just lick him. (Biggar, as qtd in "Best and Worst Dressed '99: Ricky Martin" 98)

It's the way he shakes his butt. (Salazar, as qtd. in Feliciano "Ricky Martin in Concert")

Electro-pelvis. (Essex)

Martin whose pelvis should be registered with NATO. (Essex)

The dancing Don Juan suddenly seduced America with his who's-that boy? performance. (Cagle "The Entertainers")

He was a hunka-hunka burnin Latino. (Browne)

These quotes illustrate the ways in which Martin becomes objectified. He is reduced to his body parts and their movements. In discussing white sexuality, Dyer quotes Bright, who writes of "white sex itself as vanilla, nothing added, 'blandness and rigidity'" (*White* 75). Through his dance and his performance of music, Martin enables borders to be blurred. Of the history of Latin music and the blurring of borders, Ana M. Lopez writes, "Latin American music and dance have been the perfect markers of the instability of borders and have served as indices of the imaginary demarcations that constitute the process whereby Self/ Nation defines itself (and is defined) in relationship to Others" (310). Martin's movements are discursively exoticized and Othered. It is, as Desmond notes, the forbidden movements and dance that have been "toned-down," "tamed," or "whitened" for mass consumption. In writing of Martin being marketed for mass consumption, I draw on the ways in which *latinidad*, as demonstrated through dance and his body, becomes homogenized or Hispanicized. Both the dance and the dancer become generic. His dance and his movements become exaggerated, blending together various aspects of Latin dance.

The mass consumption and the whitewashing of sexuality is illustrated by references to Salt Lake City, Utah, which run through several articles describing Martin's discursive crossover. In each of these articles Salt Lake City comes to symbolize whiteness. It is the extreme end of the discursive crossover. The sentiment exists that if Martin can make it there, he can make it anywhere. A small narrative is created from this Salt Lake City crossover. It is as follows:

> A funny thing happened last week in Salt Lake City, Utah. After Ricky Martin's
> electrifying rendition of La Copa de la Vida performed the musical equivalent of CPR
> on a listless Grammy Awards telecast in Los Angeles, fans descended on Salt Lake's
> record stores and picked the shelves clean of the Latin singer's albums. Runs on his
> albums were reported in L.A. and Miami too, but none was more surprising than the
> one in Salt Lake, a town better known for its allegiance to the Osmand Brothers that
> its enthusiasm for Latin pop. (Thigpen 80)

Through his sexuality (his exaggerated pelvic and hip movements) Martin penetrates the whiteness that stands as a barrier for Latina/os in the United States of America and the whiteness of "white-as-snow Salt Lake City" (Pellegrini "America Goes *Mucho Loco*").

Of the ways in which dance penetrates boundaries and the consumption of Others Lopez writes, "Latin American music and dance have been used by 'others' to collapse such markers of national differences. Thus 'Latin music' in the United States has often existed in a colonialist vacuum as a catchall category that collapses all the carefully nurtured nationalist origins of specific rhythms" (311). What is left is a homogenized Latin music that continues to be present and that serves as a bridge. Of this presence, Lopez notes, "The rhythm must stand in as that much which has *always* been part of the national imagination, but it must also serve as that which can performatively interpellate social actors into a community at the present" (311). Such is the case with Ricky Martin and his enactment of dance and music. He becomes the link. At one of his performances Martin made the following declaration when speaking of Venezuelan liberator Simon Bolivar: "One of his dreams was to unite the Americas and we're going to do that tonight" (Cagle "The Entertainers"). Martin positions himself as Anzaldúa's bridge ("Bridge, Drawbridge, Sandbar" 223). Interestingly, the previously mentioned Salt Lake City narrative crosses ethnic lines as well. While it appears in popular press such as *Time*, it also appears in *Hispanic*. Salt Lake City becomes a universally recognized point of whiteness for both Latina/os and white Americans. His success there becomes significant in that it is marked in both communities and referenced as a point of his entrance into the U.S. public's acceptance.

The narrative illustrates the way Martin through his embodiment and performance of accessible "safe" Other sexuality metaphorically serves as a bridge between communities. Verbally acknowledging this role and performing it, Martin offers his body up as a site of controversy. Martin agrees to act as a hybrid. The bridge must be ambiguous so as to serve as a point of identification for both of the communities he seeks to bring together. Martin uses his body to perform and disidentify within the Latin lover role that he plays with his dance and his body alterations. This accessing of a well-known stereotype allows Martin to reach white Americans with a recognizable script, while his exaggeration and resistance of it alters scripts of *latinidad* similar to practices by Carmelita Tropicana. Through his performance and embodiment of *mestizaje* Martin remains simultaneously white and Other, a bridge between multiple communities.

The Media's Ricky: Uncovering Ambiguity

When probing the ways the media in the United States has constructed Ricky Martin, one theme consistently arises: the questioning of Martin's sexual orientation and the resulting ambiguity of these questions. In examining these issues I first observe the ways in which the media has addressed questions concerning Martin's sexual orientation and its ambiguity. I will then discuss the ways in which Martin constructs ambiguity and how this ambiguity functions as a survival strategy.

The Need to Know: Manufacturing Ambiguity

His equal-opportunity appeal has sparked is-he-or-isn't-he watercooler debates.

(Essex)

In writing of one of Martin's contemporaries, Enrique Iglesias, one writer notes, "Move over, Ricky Martin! It's a hot Latin lover without sexual ambiguity" ("V-Day" 13). In this simple pronouncement the writer marks the key issues surrounding Martin: his tweaking of the Latin lover role and of his ambiguity. It is that ambiguity and the "is he or isn't he" debate that has characterized much of the media's coverage of Martin.

One strategy used to create ambiguity in the press is through the linking of Martin with other celebrities who have been known for their sexual ambiguity. The most blatant of these comparisons is offered by Melanie Feliciano: "Ricky is like Prince, Madonna and Michael Jackson—he appeals to all ages, races, cultures and sexual orientations. His sexual ambiguity, to be sure, is his ticket into the club." It is this mass appeal that makes Martin both everything and nothing. Other comparisons come a little more indirectly, such as those that proclaim, "Martin may be the Latin George Michael" ("*El Mundo*

Loves Ricky") and "Like a blond-highlighted cross between Tom Cruise and Montgomery Clift" (Essex). Richard Dyer notes that in many photographs Montgomery Clift personifies the sad young man and serves as a figure of gay identification (*The Matter of Images* 44). The image of the gay man as young and sad is an image evident in Martin's styling in the images used in his album cover art. Dyer writes, "The sad young man is neither androgynously in-between the genders nor playing with the signs of gender. His relationship to masculinity is more difficult, and thus sad" (*The Matter of Images* 42). The referencing of Martin with these people, as well as this image, helps to create and maintain ambiguity.

However, the comparisons to Cruise and Clift pale in comparison with the constant criticisms and controversies that have followed George Michael, the other celebrity to which Martin is often referenced. Having been a popular singer and sex symbol in the 1980s and 1990s, Michael was constantly asked the sexual orientation question. Initially he did not answer this question. However, when arrested for sexual behavior in a men's restroom in a public park on April 7, 1998, Michael was outed (Weider). Since this incident, which Michael characterizes as entrapment, he has spoken publicly about his sexual orientation. Of the constant questions and the press's desire to know, Michael comments, "But the press tries to make you answer to them and to the public all the time. So, I had this thing of, 'Fuck you! I'm not going to give you my private life! I'm just trying to work it out myself, thank you very much!'" (as qtd. in Weider 30). Michael's answer sounds strikingly similar to an answer given by Martin in a Barbara Walters interview and a press quote in the story by Jess Cagle: "Yes, the questions about his sexual orientation are starting to get to him. 'What I want to say sometimes is "Dude, when's the last time you f----ed your wife?"'" ("The Entertainers"). In another interview Martin states, "What I say about sexuality is, I leave it for my room and lock the door" (as qtd. in Griffiths 31). The need to know becomes overwhelming as private lives are open to public consumption. The link with Michael provides Martin with an ambiguous counterpart, a reference point for the American public. The reference to Michael operates similarly to an allusion or marks intertexuality. Even in *The Advocate* references to Michael exist in the Martin story: "George Michael's career track hasn't seemed to completely derail since his unplanned, law enforcement outing in 1998. ... [Elton] John and Michael are past the Fabian phase. ... 'There are no examples of an openly gay heartthrob appealing to teenage girls, and no one wants to test that'" (Soler, as qtd. in Griffiths 35).

Both Ricky Martin's and George Michael's looks and images have been open to interpretation. Michael comments on his look at the time of his participation in the group Wham! with Andrew Rigley, "Andrew and I didn't realize how homoerotic our image was. We had leather jackets; we had these cuffed jeans. We just thought it was cool. Andrew was the stylist— ironic that it was the straight one that was doing the styling!" (as qtd. in Weider 36). Similarly, an article in *The Advocate* ties Martin's look to gay culture:

> His whole look, the leather pants and posing with the best of what he's got, are absolutely borrowed from gay culture. ... It's a larger-than-life look that started in the gay discos in Puerto Rico and the mainstream grabbed. Look at all the Mexican boy groups. They wear eyeliner, but they're worked out. It's sensitive and macho and that's the image Ricky's built too. (Alfaro, as qtd. in Griffiths 36)

Discursively positioning Martin with Michael allows for explorations of ambiguity. Drawing a parallel between Michael's process of coming out and Martin's coming to celebrity and the ways in which he chooses to answer questions about his sexual orientation lays out a path for the reader, a reference point or discursive marker.

Others allude to Martin's sexuality more blatantly rather than simply relying on parallels and comparisons. Cagle describes Martin as "the dancing Don Juan [who] suddenly seduced America with his who's-that boy? performance" ("The Entertainers"). In using the word "boy" the writer selects a highly coded word. He alludes to a youthful or new sexuality. Furthermore, this boy motif is frequently used when Martin's innocent life as an altar boy is referenced (Griffiths 31). Andrew Essex, in "Not So Little Ricky," alludes to Martin's cross-appeal in the following way: "The next morning, women and gay men across the nation awoke and wondered: Why don't I know this guy?" The noting that Martin's fans are both male and female seems to be a common tactic for maintaining or working through ambiguity. For example, David Wild from *Rolling Stone* asks, "I keep running into women and men with crushes on you. ... Do you enjoy this sort of universal impact?" (as qtd. in Griffiths 28). Still others are more blatant: "MTV personality Serena Altschul prodded the charmer about romance in an on-camera interview: 'I'm open to love,' Martin said. 'Male or female?' Altschul tossed. Suddenly sounding like a Jeopardy contestant, the Latin wonder responded, 'Let's go for girls'" (as qtd. in Griffiths 31). Martin's sexual orientation becomes a game to the press as they compete in "who can out him first."

Some writers feel the need to challenge Martin's ambiguity more blatantly through attempts to deconstruct his words. Cagle writes:

> The big screen would be a fine place for Martin, who might prefer to be viewed in only two dimensions. ... Not only does his sex life cause consternation among fans. He speaks of a "higher power," of a time when he was "confused," of his quest for "serenity," and of his backpacking trips to seek solitude in India—all of which only tighten the riddle of who he really is beneath the gleaming exterior. ("The Entertainers")

Cagle alludes to some hidden or sinister aspect of Martin beyond the public view. Others challenge Martin in more direct and offensive ways, such as David Holthouse, who describes his feelings after one of Martin's performances. As he exits the arena he is offered a sample of fruit from a sponsor of Martin's tour: " 'Would you like a sample of a fruit square?' I was asked. 'Thanks,' I said. 'I just had one'" (Holthouse 6). Another example of a challenge to Martin's persona comes from gossip columnist Michael Musto in *The Village Voice*. Musto writes, "Ricky Martin, please stop with the girlfriend talk, girlfriend!" (as qtd. in Griffiths 35). This issue of public challenges is also addressed by George Michael when asked, "Did the gay community appear to be annoyed with you for not coming out?" (Weider 32). Michael responds, "Boy George—since Wham!—has been trying to out me. ... He was always saying horrible things ... he said that I thought I was too good for the gay community" (as qtd. in Weider 32).

Though questions remain about Martin's ambiguity in relation to his sexual orientation, there are no questions when it comes to the sex appeal inherent in his persona as he becomes defined by his body parts rather than as a whole person. Frequent references to pelvis thrusts and gyrating hips place Martin as an object of desire.

Martin is further exoticized and Othered in the larger descriptions of the Latin Explosion. First the term explosion is very sexually loaded, as noted by the play of words in *Esquire* ("There's a Latin Explosion in My Pants"). For example, discursively Martin is also positioned as Other in the title of an article discussing the Latin Explosion: "Spicing the Mix: Latino Pop Prepares to Take On America" (Cindy Rodriguez). Coupled with those who have termed the movement as an invasion (Cagle; Pellegrini; Scheerer), Latin artists are naturally positioned as foreign despite the fact that many are born in the United States and are American (Cepeda *"Mucho Loco"*; "Columbus Effects"). The discursive framework positions the crossover as dangerous and therefore difficult to accomplish.

Martin becomes an object to be accessed, leered at, and lusted over. He feels the gaze of the white American public, yet like Dyer's male pinups he returns that gaze. Dyer writes of the celebrity male pin-up and the reversal of gaze:

> Images of men aimed at women—whether star portraits, pin-ups, or drawings and paintings of men are in a particularly interesting relation to these eye contact patterns. A certain instability is produced—the first of several we encounter when looking at images of men that are offered as sexual spectacle. On one hand, this is a visual medium, these men are there to be looked at by women. On the other hand, this does violence to the codes of who looks and who is looked at (and how), and some attempt is instinctively made to counteract this violation. (*Only Entertainment* 104)

Dyer further notes that the male pinup stares back, surpassing boundaries that enclose the female when she gazes (*Only Entertainment* 109). He examines the instability of the male pinup in the contradiction of being looked at while denying it (109). Male and female power are at stake (109). Dyer explains that the male pinup is taut, ready, and poised for action (110). In one such photograph, a long-haired, shirtless Martin lies on a rock and gazes to the side as the wind blows his hair and his loose-fitting pants slip a little past his waist (Raso 25).

Through the playing of the "is he or isn't he" game, the press constructs an ambiguous sexuality for Martin. This game allows for the public spectacle and competition of who will out him first. Martin becomes a "perfect" sexual object who smiles through the photograph as he points his index finger into a space beyond the photograph while a larger-than-life photograph of himself looms in the background (Rene Cruz 46–47).

Questions of Sexuality

> If one's own identity is always and necessarily complex, compound, and multifaceted, if one's own intentions are therefore somewhat ambiguous, even to one's own self; and if one's own self, and its effects, are therefore multiply refracted in the world of others, then one can hardly expect less from others.
>
> (Lancaster 14)

In writing of the transvestitism of everyday life, Lancaster indexes an experience similar to that of the many *mestizo* people—the complexity inherent in the origin of oneself and the projection of oneself. It is this complexity that Martin accesses in his performances, his embodiment of *latinidad* and the issues regarding his sexual orientation. In his interviews, music, and performances

Martin creates an ambiguity that serves as a means of survival. As previously discussed Martin becomes a bridge. Of this ambiguity Lancaster writes, "In such moments, identity, identification, and intention are simultaneously revealed, concealed, performed, manipulated, and denied" (Lancaster 14). Martin enacts ambiguity in interviews and ambiguity through the use of archetype. In this section I discuss the ways in which ambiguity functions as a means of disidentification or survival. Though Fernando Delgado and I have previously discussed this tactic, I use this space to further elaborate upon Martin's strategies.

In examining Ricky Martin's voice and the resulting discursive creation of ambiguity I focus on several interviews but draw primarily on his two interviews with Barbara Walters. The first interview is from *Barbara Walters' 10 Most Fascinating People of 1999* and the second is *The Barbara Walters Special*. In each of these interviews Martin maintains ambiguity with regard to his sexual orientation. As scenes of Martin dancing flash across the screen, Walters speaks in a voice-over, "Not since Elvis have a pair of hips caused so much excitement." Walters begins the interview and as Martin sings a chorus of "Maria" in Spanish, she pants, "more more more more." Immediately, the subject of Martin's sexuality comes to the forefront:

Barbara Walters: You know much of the attention on you has been focused on your sex appeal and Gloria Estefan told you to enjoy your sexuality, what does that mean?

Ricky Martin: Gloria told me enjoy it while you have it. It's not going to be always. Enjoy it. You're Latin. Don't be ashamed of it enjoy it.

BW: Tell me how you're enjoying it. What are you doing about enjoying it?

RM: I live la vida loca.

BW: There are so many young women and so many not so young women (*cough cough*) who want to know are you involved with anyone right now?

RM: (*Looks off to the side pensively, shakes his head and slowly answers*) Yeah.

BW: Tell me more. Are you in love?

RM: (*Quickly answers*) No.

BW: Have you been really in love?

RM: I've been in love. (*Martin gets a distant far off look, his face drops.*)

BW: Your face just changed.

RM: It hurts.

BW: She didn't want you? Somebody turned you down?

RM: Yeah.

BW: How old were you?

RM:	I was 21 years old.
BW:	Ugh and she broke your heart.
RM:	I said I will never love that same way again. What a liar.

Walters marks Martin's sexuality, while he neither confirms nor denies it. Walters casts Martin as a sexual object and Latin lover through her overtures, flirting, and request that he speak to her in Spanish. Martin enacts this stereotype as he mentions his *latinidad*, living *la vida loca*, and romantic love. Walters presents him with the Latin lover (Hispanic) script and he accepts. She asserts the heterosexuality of that model, but Martin uses a disidentification strategy by working within the script and out of it at the same time by remaining sexually ambiguous.

This ambiguity was also present in a June 1999 America Online chat. Fielding questions from subscribers, Martin is asked, "Do you believe in love at first sight?" Ambiguity is coded when Martin answers, "Yes, I have had love at first sight. ... The spiritual aspect for me in a person is so important. I go after a person who is balanced and serene and in control of her feelings and actions. That's what really turns me on, someone who knows what she wants in life and is not compulsive" ("AOL Chat" June 5, 1999). Martin plays the pronoun game, remaining ambiguous while simultaneously asserting an attraction for the opposite sex. In another interview with *Rolling Stone*, Martin expresses a similar ambiguity: "When I do music I don't focus on just women or men. ... I want to see the guy bringing his girlfriend to the show and enjoying the music with her. I don't want to see only girls. It's going to sound weird, but that's not the turn-on I'm looking for" (as qtd. in Griffiths 32). Martin's strategy of remaining sexually ambiguous shows the ways in which he works within the dominant script of the Latin lover, disidentifying with it by choosing an ambiguous sexuality, expanding the notion of the Latin lover (Delgado and Calafell). Munoz writes, "Disidentification is a performative mode of tactical recognition that various minoritarian subjects employ in an effort to resist the oppressive and normalizing discourse of dominant ideology" (*Disidentifications* 97). Martin's disidentification is similar to that of Cuban performance artist Carmelita Tropicana; Muñoz writes of "her over-the-top 'exoticism,' her deep investment in gaudy and toxic stereotypes of the Latina, her red feather boas, and the occasional splash of glitter that might punctuate her performances" (*Disidentifications* xiii–xiv). Similar to Tropicana, Martin's Latin lover is the over-the-top stereotype that allows him to disidentify and alter, working both on and against this racist ideology. Muñoz argues these acts are powerful because they are "reformulating the world *through* the performance of politics" (*Disidentifications* xiv).

Prior to the *The Barbara Walters Special* that aired before the 2000 Academy Awards, Walters had revealed on her daytime show *The View* that indeed she was asking Martin the question everyone wanted an answer to, whether he is gay. Furthermore, Walters bragged that he answered the question. As the interview begins the voice-over starts and images of a dancing Martin flash. Martin and Walters walk on the edge of the ocean, arm in arm and with their shoes off. Martin is tan, taut, and beautiful, glowing in a white T-shirt and lime-green cover shirt. Walters is lost in the moment. The following is a transcript of the portion of the *The Barbara Walters Special* interview during which Walters launches her "interrogation":

BW: When did you so to speak become a man?

RM: I was fourteen years old.

BW: Good experience?

RM: It was not what I expected.

BW: Ricky when you have the kind of stardom that you have the rumors follow. And with you there have been the rumors that question or talk about your sexual orientation. You must be aware of these rumors.

RM: Of course.

BW: Okay. Do they hurt? How do you handle them?

RM: The worst has been intimacy. Sometimes I go, "Well if it's going to sell some albums, why not, you can say anything you want." But I know how this works, I have been in the business for seventeen years. And I know how it works.

BW: How does it work?

RM: Well some … when they have … sometimes some people in the media when they have nothing to say they invent things. I'm not concerned about my reaction. I'm concerned with my peoples' reactions. Like my nieces they go to school and start reading things. My mom goes to the beauty parlor and. … Sexuality and homosexuality should not be a problem for anybody. I think that sexuality is something that each individual should deal with in their own way. And that's all I have to say about that.

BW: Well, you could stop these rumors. You could say as many artists have. Yes I am gay or no I'm not.

RM: I understand Barbara.

BW: But it's in your power to do.

RM: Thank you so much for giving me …

BW: But I'm bringing it up Ricky because you know that this is being said and you are even being named.

RM: I know and I understand. And thank you so much for giving me the opportunity to express the rumors. … But for some reason I just don't feel like it. (sic)

BW: You know that I respect that because you have allowed me to bring it up and I
    respect that at this point you don't want to deal with it.
RM: It is something so mine. I give it all when I am on stage. I give it all in interviews.
    But you've gotta keep something for yourself sometimes. And it's for me.
BW: Could the rumors hurt you professionally?
RM: I don't think professionally. No it's more about the talent than who do you go to
    bed with.
BW: Of course on the other hand as you said. If gay people think you are gay and
    straight people think you are straight, hey if it means a bigger audience.
RM: Exactly, I really don't have a problem. I respect everybody and that's all I want.
    I want people to respect me … the same way.

Clearly Martin illustrates that he knows the power of naming. A power struggle emerges as Walters attempts to corner Martin, wearing him down bit by bit. Martin remains staunchly, discursively ambiguous, yet his features betray him. The emotional content from his answers is read on his face. As he states that his sexuality is something so his that he does not feel like addressing the rumors, and that he cannot be hurt professionally, Martin remains ambiguous. In his answers he disidentifies. Muñoz alludes to this ambiguity when he writes, "Disidentification is a third mode of dealing with dominant ideology, one that neither opts to assimilate within such a structure nor strictly oppose it; rather, disidentification is a strategy that works on and against dominant ideology" (11). Martin disidentifies against ideology that maintains binaries—ideology that creates either/or in regards to sexuality. Martin refuses to submit to the binary that Walters tries to force on him. His refusal to answer can be read in several ways. First, he may be a heterosexual who does not want to eliminate his gay fan base through the renouncing of ambiguity. Second, he may simply desire not to give into the media's consumption. Third, he may want to remain ambiguous rather than being forced out. In the end of this power struggle it is Martin who seizes the power back from Walters as she attempts to force him to name himself.

I further liken Martin's performance to the strategy of deflection used by Ellen DeGeneres, in which there is no clear identification with either homosexuality or heterosexuality (Shugart 39). Shugart argues that Ellen performs this strategy by "dramatizing her awkwardness and lack of savvy regarding sex" (39). Negrón-Muntaner writes that Martin cultivates an image of being married to his career. I see this as his part of his strategy of deflection. He constructs a narrative of being overwhelmed with the demands of his stardom, yet at the same time, because of this vast public exposure, he must keep his sexuality private.

Creating Ambiguity through Archetype

In his music Martin embodies an ambiguous persona who is a creation of the alternation of the Latin lover script, an acceptable and well-known Hispanic script (Delgado and Calafell). Perhaps one of the best illustrations of Ricky Martin's embodiment of the Latin lover character is evidenced in his performance of the song "Shake Your Bon-Bon." His songwriters, Robi Rosa, George Noriega, and Desmond Child, write lyrics playing up this image while Martin enacts the role through his body and voice. In the lyrics Martin directly references a hyper-sexuality prominent within the Latin lover role. This exaggerated sexuality, this caricature, embodied by Martin's exaggerated hip movements as he performs the song alongside his scantily clad dancers, creates for Martin a space to work in within and out of the stereotype. Martin does this movement within and out of the stereotype by specifically alluding to the Latin lover script, one of the few scripts acceptable by the white imagination, "yet at the same time disidentifying with it through spectacle" (Delgado and Calafell 235). Martin mocks the accepted scripts, describing himself as a desperado/Latin lover singing for sex underneath his lover's window (Rosa, Noreiga, and Child). In referencing the narrative of Romeo and Juliet, Martin disidentifies with a well-known script, and it is campy. Within the lyrics Martin directly references another Latino stereotype of hyper-masculinity: the desperado or bandit. Interestingly, this same imagery and character has been adopted within the sphere of Chicano rap, a clearly masculine and misogynist space (Delgado "Chicano Ideology Revisited"). Martin creates and embodies spectacle, an over-the-top Latin lover who reminds us that "no matter who acts them out, such performative performances can never simply *imitate* or *mimic* some original practice, person, or type, for they are always *in excess* of their target. That is what distinguishes them as 'performances'" (Lancaster 14). Martin clearly acts in excess of the Latin lover role, thus allowing him to disidentify from it and refuse to be pulled into the ideology that guides it. Martin uses spectacle as a means of survival.

Strengthening his alteration of the Latin lover role, Martin calls upon its counterpart—the Hispanic vamp. The vamp is motivated by sex and desire (Keller). She is evil and cunning, and she is often driven by a fetish for white men. Castillo notes the connection of this character with witch, or *bruja*, imagery and mysticism ("The Distortion of Desire" 147). This vamp image as well as the counterpart virgin image have roots in historical and cultural contexts of Malinche, La Virgen de Guadalupe, and La Llorona. Each of these images is important and needs to be examined because Martin uses them in his music. The most extreme case of this dichotomy are the songs "Livin' la Vida Loca" and "She's All I Ever Had."

Within "Livin' la Vida Loca" several key themes present in the vamp archetype quickly come to surface. First, there is the allure of the physical. In the imaginations of white males, Latinas are seen as highly exotic and erotic sexualized beings. Beyond the allure of the physical, Martin sings of another type of allure, a rumored hidden, exoticized sexuality that Latin women possess. Martin alludes directly to this sexuality when he sings of the ways in which the woman makes him lose control, evidenced by his waking in a strange place with his money gone. Like the cunning vamp continually presented (Rosa and Child), the woman referenced in the song is cunning and manipulative. This manipulation is consistent with vamp themes discussed by Keller. This loss of control indicates a deviance or a danger that must be stopped. A loss of control means a loss of power, a danger to Latino sexuality and masculinity. Working hand in hand with the loss of control is the allusion to the Latina as being evil or defiant of the virgin/whore dichotomy. This image of the evil woman is consistent with the stories of La Llorona and La Malinche. The positioning of the woman in the song as exotic, dangerous, or evil is alluded to when Martin describes her affinity for the supernatural and her devil red lips. Her dangerous sexuality leads men to powerlessness and loss of control.

Juxtaposed to the vamp imagery is the virgin. The virgin is featured most prominently in the song "She's All I Ever Had." (Though the videos to these songs are not specifically named as text, it is interesting to note the ways in which the visual representations of each woman affirm their positions as vamp and whore: one scantily dressed; the other in white.) In the song the woman becomes a site of Martin's redemption and self-exploration. She loses her personhood and is instead positioned as an object of redemption, a theme consistent with the virgin or self-sacrificing senorita. The woman in the song is discursively placed on the margins, while the sensations she evokes are centered. What she does for the man, rather than herself, is of importance. The woman becomes a means to access these emotions. Her importance lies in the way she helps the male to feel about himself. The purity of the woman is valorized because, through purity, the male finds a way to affirm his own identity. If she were not so pure, would the male still feel the same way about himself? She becomes a reference point or marker for his esteem and a trophy to his manhood. This is similar to the discussion by Stavans, who writes of the way that female sexuality is sacrificed for masculinity. Also of note is the way in which Martin's use of the dichotomy allows him to access masculinities or conceptions of machismo as described by Mirandé. Martin allows himself to be positioned as hot-blooded, sexual, or macho while simultaneously enacting the role of considerate and caring macho. Adopting both the Latin lover and the vamp script allows Martin to disidentify with the Latin lover script and the larger script of Hispanic homogenization. By choosing not to remain true to the script of Latin lover and instead altering it, Martin resists interpellation into racist ideologies that delimit Latina/o identity. Through his embodiment he forces new, less restrictive scripts. In writing of camp, Muñoz recognizes the importance of recitation and citation in its performance in that it can challenge dominant meanings. In altering and performing these well-known scripts, Martin enacts camp as a disidentification, a survival strategy. Martin to a lesser extent parallels some of the camp strategies performed by Carmelita Tropicana (Muñoz *Disidentification* 128).

Also important in examining the scripts that Martin employs is his role as advocate for Puerto Rico. Much news coverage was centered around Martin's meeting with President Clinton to discuss U.S. test bombing on Puerto Rico's island of Vieques. Of the bombing Martin commented, "What are we going to do? Because it's impossible for my land to be under so much stress because of this" ("Ricky Martin to Ask Clinton to Withdraw from Vieques"). Martin characterized his position as more humanitarian than political, noting, "Puerto Rico is united in this cause and I'm a part of it" (Wolk *"La Vida Vota"*; Ives "Ricky Martin Urges President Clinton to Halt Bombing Practice"). Martin's advocacy was characterized in the following way: "See how easy it is to meet with the President? Maybe if the American farmers learned how to swivel their hips and got themselves a hit single, they'd make better lobbyists" (Wolk *"La Vida Vota"*). It seems to be difficult to see Martin without his heightened sexuality. Considering the way Martin disidentifies from the Latin lover script, his role as advocate or diplomat seems to again alter various scripts and enact ambiguity. Martin has been characterized as a beautiful sex object. For him to perform as something other than that disrupts the essentialism and the stereotyping that has constantly framed his representations.

Ambiguity: A Privileged Practice

In this chapter I have attempted to create a more complex picture of Ricky Martin and his importance in popular culture, particularly in the moment of the Latin Explosion. In discussing Martin's ability to pass into the terrain of whiteness and his middle space of sexuality, it becomes clear that his ability to perform ambiguity is in a large part a matter of privilege. *Mestizaje* has its benefits for Martin because he is light. Martin's entrance onto the popular culture radar was largely due to his whiteness (Negrón-Muntaner). These are undeniably the racial politics in the United States, but we must go a step further to ask what happens in these spaces that Others are invited/permitted to cross over or pass through.

In Martin's case the invitation allowed whites to gaze upon and desire his fetishized body in the quest to get a bit of the Other. However, it also enabled resistive performances that challenged binaries of race in the United States and sexuality. In American popular culture essentialist scripts are what are used for making sense of the Other or the "foreign." Deviation from these scripts is often punished. Scripts are defined, redefined, and refined until they become acceptable to the dominant culture (Sloop). Ricky Martin has found a way to work within these problematic scripts, defying them while simultaneously enacting them. When examining Ricky Martin, I reflect on a statement by Karen Christian: "The hypermasculinity and hyperfemininity of these characters (their excess) makes them resemble drag performers whose objective is to produce convincing gender illusions" (75). Through exaggeration, ambiguity, and spectacle Martin enacts a survival strategy while creating a space of resistance. By remaining sexually ambiguous Martin both plays the game and defies it. Martin "works on and against dominant ideology," neither assimilating nor opposing it (Muñoz *Disidentification* 11). He becomes a symbol of *mestizaje*, an illustration of continuums and alternatives modes of thinking not embraced in the United States.

Postscript: A Love Letter and Performance in Honor of Ricky

Dear Ricky,

I write you this letter not really knowing if you will even get it, but because I need to think through some things in my journey to recover you and myself. A funny thing started to happen to me a while back. How do I explain this coherently? Okay, do you remember when we were spending every day together in the spring of 2000? You were so hot and so was Marc [Anthony]. It was like you were everywhere and everyone kept asking me what I thought of your popularity. Frankly, at times it was overwhelming! Well a funny thing started to happen; it was right around that following November actually. I remember I got up early one morning because I knew your new CD was being released and I was determined to be there to get it (you even had a free promotional calendar—it was great!). So I got your CD and listened to it and something was just not the same—yeah, you had the song "She Bangs" and the hot video, but some of the luster was gone. Then I started to get all these questions from people such as, "What happened to Ricky Martin?" or "His new CD isn't doing too well, what's going on?" I felt like I had to continually justify or explain your situation to everyone. Never mind that you have been an international superstar for years before releasing your English-language album, all anyone cared about was your U.S. success and the so-called Latin Explosion/Invasion you were credited with starting. I know I am preaching to the choir!!!!!!!!!!

So all these questions got me thinking. Why should I have to justify your success or lack of it? Okay, maybe I am being over dramatic, but why do we always blame the victim instead of the system? This problem has been on my mind for some time, especially when I look around and continue to see the way our culture is commodified for the masses and then easily discarded when the fad passes. I mean where does that leave us, and how does making our culture a fetish make our lives any easier? These were all questions that continued to bother me. Actually, they angered me. What made me even angrier was that when I was supposed to present a paper at my national conference a while back on *Latingirl Magazine* (the teen magazine for "Hispanic" girls) I found out that the magazine had gone out of business. Again this was a symptom of the Latin Explosion and mainstream U.S. obsession with cultural tourism. What I ended up doing at the conference was writing a paper that discussed this issue and argued for a revision of ways to view "the text" in rhetorical criticism with a focus on process rather than product, essentially situating the importance of context through the realms of performance and media studies. I was really happy, but I don't think everyone got it.

Okay, Ricky I know I am digressing a bit so I will come back to you. So, I have been thinking a lot about this radical street performance I did in your honor a while back. I know you are probably looking at this letter and saying, "Radical street performance? What is that?" Well let me tell you. I read this book edited by this Jan Cohen-Cruz and she describes street performance in the following way: "By *radical* I refer to acts that question or re-envision ingrained social arrangements of power. *Street* signals theatrics that take place in public by-ways with minimal constraints on access. *Performance* here indicates expressive behavior intended for public viewing" (1). Ricky you are my contested reality! The Latin Explosion is my contested reality—I was trying to get people to change their scripts. I guess part of the reasons why I have decided to engage this issue is not just because of the reasons I have already described, but because it hurts. I know this sounds flaky, but it hurts to see your culture abused, worn by others as ornamental, simplified, degraded, devalued, misunderstood, and then discarded. So basically what was at stake is my livelihood and dignity. I remember when I lost the most tangible aspect of my culture—my grandfather. The loss was immense. In a similar manner, it hurts each time our cultures are popularized and then discarded. Do you remember how you felt when Selena died? Is everyone dying to cross over or do we have to die to cross over. I remember one of my professors at Arizona State University wrote this essay about the film *Showdown in Little Tokyo* and he made a comment about the expendability of Asian bodies in popular culture.[1] He said something to the effect that dead Asian bodies are everywhere. Sometimes I think dead Latina/o bodies are everywhere—by bodies, I mean the physical bodies as well as the artifacts of our culture. So do you understand what is at stake here and why this is a contested reality? I mean, you and I might see what is happening, but does everyone else? It's kind of like something I read in the Cohen-Cruz book—this idea of bearing witness. When someone bears witness to something it means that you are "publicly illuminating a social act that one does not know how to change but at least must acknowledge" (Cohen-Cruz 5). There were some examples of this such as Diana Taylor's "Making a Spectacle: The Mothers of the Plaza de Mayo" and Marguerite Walker's "Border *Boda* or Divorce *Fronterizo?*" In the case discussed by Taylor the mothers were mourning their missing children by using placards and placing pictures onto their bodies in a public place to protest, while in the case discussed by Walker protestors literally illuminated an alarming situation. In both of these cases there was an issue or crisis that had no easy answer but definitely needed to be acknowledged and addressed. But beyond the idea of bearing witness I also want to get people to see that I was doing as a critique of the everyday or taken granted. It is kind of like this idea of integration Cohen-Cruz talks about: "The insertion of theatrically heightening scenario into people's everyday lives to provide an emotional experience of what might otherwise remain distant" (5). I know I am being really vague right now, but I think once I tell you the specifics of my performance you will understand why I have told you about these two types of street performance.

Okay, so having shared my sadness and burden, I want to share my joy in exposing this situation. After choosing a topic, the next logical step was to choose a space. So where does a lot of this commodification take place? What are Latina/os valued for? Well, you know Ricky, as people of color we obviously have rhythm, right? So you know we will be valued for our entertainment skills. Latinas have always been valued for our bodies, never our ideas—just look at all the hoopla around J-Lo's butt. Considering a site I thought about how Cohen-Cruz described the goal of radical street performance: "Radical street performance strives to transport everyday reality to something more ideal" (1). Okay, so how can I transport everyday reality into something more? Thinking about the site more I reflected on something else Cohen-Cruz said, that radical street performance was "a bridge between imagined and real actions, often facilitated by taking place at the very sites that the performance markers want transformed" (1). The performance should ideally take place at a space that I want transformed, so I came to the conclusion that the best place would be in front of the *Wherehouse* music store on Franklin Street. Where else could I go to buy some Latin culture and then trade it back used for a new piece when I was done? It was perfect. But this site wasn't enough; something else had to be done. So I considered my body.

I need to start a new paragraph here because you know where this is going. To steal a phrase from Betty Friedan, it's "the problem that has no name." It's the problem of marking an "ethnic" body. For years our bodies have been consumed and displayed in popular culture as "Brown" bodies, so much that we have sometimes come to believe in these images despite the diversity in our culture. It's kind of like strategic essentialism. During the Chicano movement it was decided that the image of the maligned dark-skinned Chicano would be celebrated because of the history of maltreatment. Everyone knew this was essentialism, but sometimes you have to strategically essentialize for political ends. The problem comes when decades later you are still doing this and now the essentialism of years ago becomes the so-called reality criteria that you use to give authenticity tests. So where am I going and how do I fit in? Well, all my life I have been the white brown girl. Do you know the fear I felt the first time I did an academic presentation about Latina/os? I was just waiting for the other Latina/os in the crowd to start throwing tomatoes at me and call me a fraud! I was terrified because I have been subjected to all these authenticity games all my life. I am always in fear of having to justify my body and myself. Why not contest this aspect of my body and its inscriptions through performance? So I put together a costume. It is a short black skirt, a black tank top, some pantyhose, a leopard coat, and platform shoes. But the clothes have been altered. My chest had a sign across it that read "Salma's breasts," while my butt had a sign that said, "J-Lo's butt." The kicker is "Guadalupe's virginity," and I don't think I need to tell you where I put that one! Other parts of my body are marked accordingly to represent Latinas who have occupied space in popular culture, each of them valued only for their bodies. So in effect I am using my body as a site to place fetishized ethnic body parts onto an "unfetishized," "unmarked," "unrecognized," ethnic body. This is complex enough, but trust me it gets worse. Cohen-Cruz writes, "Space is always controlled by *someone* and exists *somewhere*, so it is inevitably marked by a particular class or race and not equally accessible to everyone" (2). Her statement reminded me of an essay by Cheris Kramarae, which I read when I was in my master's program. But what Kramarae argues is that public space is male space; therefore, men feel they have the right to harass women who enter their domain. So in a sense bringing my highly sexualized and ethnically contested body into this space serves to complicate things even more!

This idea of public space is also similar to some of the tactics discussed by Lauren Berlant and Elizabeth Freeman in their essay "Queer Nationality." Describing the multiple tactics of Queer Nation, Berlant and Freeman unpack the ways that the in-your-face politics of Queer Nation contest what is held as public space and bring private identities into official spectacle (137). But what Queer Nation also seems to do is appropriate the popular and at times reappropriate it. For example, Berlant and Freeman talk about "Gay Bart." A practice of Queer Nation is to take a corporate strategy to "exploit the psychic unboundedness of consumers who depend upon products to articulate, produce, and satisfy their desires" (136). Thus, taking someone like Bart Simpson allows them to examine how Bart's "unboundedness as a commodity identity exploits the way that the fantasy of being something else merges with the stereotype to confer an endlessly shifting series of identities upon the consumer's bodies" (137). Another particularly charming tactic was to change the "p" in the Gap ads to "y," which "outs" the gap for appropriating and commodifying the style of gay-coded clothing to sell to the mainstream. The thing that is so attractive about each of these strategies is that they work within this idea of hidden in plain sight. It is kind of like illuminating or lifting the veil of false consciousness or problematizing the familiar. That's what I want to do with my performance: problematize the everyday or taken for granted—whether it be public space, popular culture, or icons.

Okay, let's get back to the good stuff—so you have the image of Bern in front of the *Wherehouse* at midday in her "excesses of *latinidad*" suit. Wow, I will be close to the street and dressed kind of risqué—will I be a streetwalker? Now you want to know where you come in right? Well in case people don't get the message from my clothes (read: Latinas in popular culture are only valued for one thing ... like Ricky they will be on their way out), they will get it when I hand out my fliers. I made them look like lost dog fliers. At the top it says "Missing." Underneath is your picture with the handwritten words, "Have you seen this man? He's been missing since the media fabricated 'Latin Invasion/Explosion of 1999–early 2000. Please don't let him become another casualty. If you have any information about his whereabouts please call The Center for the Recuperation of Commodified, Commercialized, and Disposed of Latina/o culture at 1-800-Get-Ricky. Still Missing: J-Lo's butt, salsa rhythms, *Latingirl Magazine*, Spanglish."

So initially when this performance started I sat on a nearby bench and then proceeded to get up and take off the leopard coat in a ceremonious fashion. My clothes were revealed and I began handing out the fliers. I tried to let my body and the flier do all the talking because I thought it would be more powerful that way. I remember reading an essay by Adrian Piper that also dealt with issues of contested bodies. It was called "Passing for White, Passing for Black." I loved it and related to it. In another essay, "Xenophobia and the Indexical Present II: Lecture," Piper writes, "An object can be a catalytic agent and can make a change in other sorts of objects without undergoing change itself" (128). Inspired by Piper's cards, which challenged people's racism in conjunction with her "unmarked" body, I looked for similar ways to use my body, the signs on it, and the fliers I handed out.

The nonverbal can do a couple of things; it can possibly communicate in more nuanced and less threatening ways. By handing people the fliers I was doing what Piper described—the flier asserted itself into the everyday (the person walking down the street) and they got to read and initiate a dialogue with me if they chose. But at least they were informed, and their everyday perception was altered, challenged, or if I'm lucky reaffirmed.

It sounds really great, right? Well, I have to tell you it was quite an experience, and the only reason I did it was because I love you so much. Believe it or not I tend to be a pretty shy person. Well, I have to tell you, it was an interesting and mixed reaction. Most of the people who took the fliers and seemed engaged were men. A lot of the women I tried to give the fliers to refused to take them. I am not quite sure what to make of all of this; perhaps it is because of the politics of the gaze and that I invited people to look at my body when I gave them the fliers. Who knows for sure, but that is my guess.

It has been a while since that performance and I have continued to think about it and of you. When I got your last album, *Live*, I noticed that you looked a lot more butch than you did before. Your clean-shaven smooth face was gone, replaced with a five-o'clock shadow. In interviews you were still coyly ambiguous but a lot more daring in describing some of your favorite sexual positions and fantasies. I was a bit surprised, but I figured you knew what you were doing because you are so good at this game. You're such a trickster.

Well, Ricky, I think that's all I really have to share right now. I hope some day that you can let me know what you think of all of this. Until then I have included a copy of a picture of myself from the street performance. Please don't laugh. Remember I did it for you.

Eternally yours,

Bern

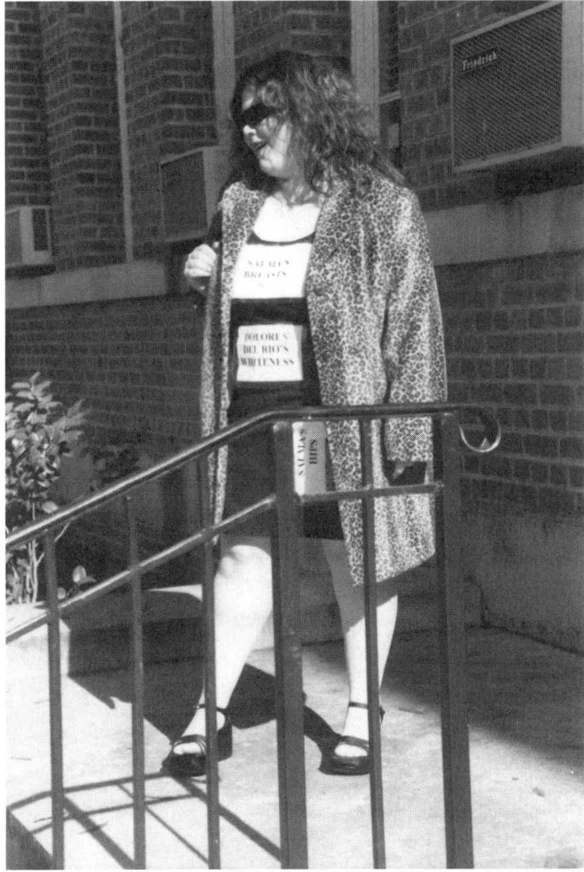

Figure 1 Bernadette Marie Calafell in radical street performance mode.

· 6 ·

REFLECTING ON THE (IM)POSSIBILITIES OF *LATINIDAD*: AFFECTIVE CONNECTIONS AMONG LATINA/OS

As I have mentioned in various chapters, over the past six years I have moved between the Southwest, Southeast, and Northeast. I have wandered between Chicana/o, Mexican American, Mexican, Latina/o, Puerto Rican, and Dominican spaces. Simultaneous with these moves has been the emergence and rise of academic discussions about the possibilities or impossibilities of *latinidad* or pan-Latina/o identities.[1] These discussions have been points of dialogue in my everyday life through my engagement with them in my classrooms and in my research.[2] My desire to participate in this conversation has largely been a selfish one motivated by my need for community. My position in these debates has shifted from initially being overly enthusiastic to being cynical, and now to being simply undecided. I desire a pan-Latina/o connection because of the political possibilities; however, I have real doubts about its feasibility because of my engagement with the literature and my personal experiences.

In early 2006 I traveled to New York City to participate in a conference about Afro-Latina/o identities and the potential of pan-Latina/o connections. As someone who has been interested in finding political points of connection across Latina/o groups for both personal and political motivations, I was excited about the possibilities that the conference might hold for thinking about alliances across Latina/o difference. I have always been committed to examining our identities as Chicanas, which includes our often silenced African ancestry, because, as Gloria Anzaldúa writes,

> Before the Chicano and the undocumented worker and the Mexican from the other side can come together, before the Chicano can have unity with Native Americans and other groups, we need to know the history of their struggle and they need to know ours. Our mothers, our sisters and brothers, the guys who hang out on street corners, the children in the playground, each of us must know our Indian lineage, our afro-*mestizaje*, our history of resistance. (*Borderlands* 108)

Following Anzaldúa's lead I excitedly enrolled in the conference. It seemed like an important event and a space for us as Latina/os to confront the racisms in our community through honest dialogue.

My goal in going to this conference was to reexamine my identity as a Chicana as a way to create bridges with other Latina/o groups. I imagined that the kind of solidarity that seemed to be hinted at in the title of the conference would be similar to Chandra Mohanty's discussion of Jodi Dean's theory of reflective solidarity, which takes the stance "I ask you to stand by me over and against a third" and, as Mohanty writes, "involves thematizing the third voice, 'to reconstruct solidarity as an inclusive ideal,' rather than as an 'us vs. them' notion" (7). I soon found out, however, that my assumptions were somewhat naïve and idealistic, as much of the conference was spent demonstrating that we had internalized a U.S.-centered way of thinking about race based on a black and white dichotomy, rather than exploring ways to make connections on the basis of our identities as Latina/os, mixed race because of colonialism and the slave trade. The very critiques we level against others in frustration were being played out all around me. The conference in my experience was not about making connections or coalition building but instead about reinforcing our differences and building walls. *Mestizaje* was a bad word at this conference, and it was quite an eye-opener for me, leaving me pretty disillusioned. This led me to question my goals in going to the conference and wondering whether in fact a political pan-Latina/o identity was indeed something to strive for, something even possible, or something even desirable.

Months after the conference I once again began to think through the possibility of pan-Latina/o connections. In pondering ways to configure pan-Latina/o connections while maintaining a respect for difference, I borrow from the underlying aims of Mohanty's idea of a "feminism without borders," a coalition that envisions change and social justice work across lines of demarcation and difference (2). Like Mohanty, "I define solidarity in terms of mutuality, accountability, and the recognition of common interests as the basis for relationships among diverse communities. ... Diversity and difference are central values here—to be acknowledged and respected, not erased in the building of alliances" (7). I do not idealize or imagine the forming of these coalitional spaces necessarily to be easy. Similarly, Anzaldúa writes,

> Alliance work is the attempt to shift position, change position, reposition ourselves regarding our individual and collective identities. In alliance we are confronted with the problem of how we share or don't share, how we can position ourselves with individuals or groups who are different from and at odds with each other, how can we reconcile one's love for diverse groups when members of these groups do not love each other, cannot relate to each other, and don't know how to work together. ("Bridge, Drawbridge" 219)

I cite Anzaldúa and Mohanty in seeking to be attentive not only to the differences that exists across Latina/o groups but also to the tensions marked by generation, language abilities, migration histories, and race, among other things. These are tensions I have witnessed and experienced first hand as I moved from Arizona to North Carolina and New York.

In looking for spaces of *latinidad* or pan-Latina/o identification, it becomes essential to deconstruct what "Latino" has come to mean in popular culture, because this is the dominant script that is presented of us and that we must negotiate in our lived experience. Thus, this project becomes about deconstructing what Latino means for those who identify with the label either by choice or by force, the meanings constructed in dominant discourses, and the various negotiations such as manifestations of pan-Latina/o connections. I am interested in the construction Latino because of its deployment in popular culture, noting, as does Sánchez, that "new identifications, even those arising out of misidentification, colonialism, and subordinate social positioning ... can serve as rallying strategies, but they can also be deployed to stigmatize and censure particular groups" (41).

In my desire to create points of connection across Latina/o groups I have taken two approaches in my work, the first of which has been to examine texts that are Latina/o in their presentation such as those of Fernando Delgado and the mass-marketed photography book *Americanos: Latino Life in the United States* or my own study of *Latina Magazine*. The second strategy has been to retheorize the ways we understand Chicana/o identities as a means of finding points of connection with other groups through affect that revolves around memory, desire, performance, and possibility. In this chapter, I chart some of the ways the discourse Latino has emerged over the past few years, follow it up with a discussion of ways that others have considered how to make connections across difference, and finally make some preliminary gestures toward the possibility of a pan-Latina/o identification through a brief discussion of dead rapper Big Punisher and Reggaeton.

The Manufacturing of Latino

As Dolores Tanno has explained, there are a plethora of names that people of Latin American descent can use to name themselves. Each of these labels differs in political orientation and ideological stance, ranging from the more assimilationist Hispanic to the politically charged ethnic-specific Chicana/o to the more recent, larger identification of Latina/o. By adding critiques of sexism to the mix, as Chicana feminists did, ways of naming ourselves became increasingly complex. Delgado complicates and challenges the neatness of labels by looking at the vernacular use of these labels in texts such as *Lowrider Magazine*, pointing to the ways that identities and labels are never clear-cut. He argues, "Latina/os can be many different things when, as subjects, they put identity terms into their everyday communication practices" ("When the Silenced Speak" 424). Within all of these discussions we can chart the ways these communities name themselves, the ways they are named by the dominant culture, and how they negotiate this relationship. For example, we can map these negotiations over time by looking at terms such as Chicana/o and Hispanic.

This negotiation has been particularly significant since the 1999–2000 media-constructed "Latin Explosion." As Alberto Sandoval-Sánchez writes, "Nineteen ninety-nine will always be remembered as the last year of the millennium when Latinos/as took over U.S. popular culture and its media" (13). In discussing the Latin Explosion/Invasion/crossover, I mark it as the moment when Latina/os gained increasing national prominence in popular culture because of Ricky Martin's shaking of his hips at the Grammys when he performed "La Copa de la Vida." Overnight, Martin created a craze, a sensation, and desire for all things Latino. Following Martin in this "crossover" were U.S.-born Latinos and Latinas such as Marc Anthony and Jennifer Lopez, who also entered under the banner of Latino, Latina, or Latin rather than Puerto Rican. As Sandoval-Sánchez writes,

This tremendous booming of Latino/a participation and visibility in the American national cultural arena entails more than a crossover into the mainstream. Neither this, nor a renaissance of an U.S. Latino/a presence in the Anglo-American cultural landscape is the outcome of spontaneous combustion, a passing trend, or a unique phenomenon. It bears witness to the fact that a demographic change has occurred, a new generation of U.S. Latinos/as has emerged, and—in a capitalist society as ours—this generation has a high consuming potential and represents a marketable target in a competitive and growing national and global economy with the movement of capital work and force. (14)

Some might argue that Chicana/Tejana singer Selena Quintanilla Perez, murdered in 1995, had reached national prominence and began the craze for all things Latino. I argue that although Selena did indeed open the door for others such as Martin and started a craze in the publishing industry for magazines geared toward Latina/os, she did not introduce the discourse of Latino into the popular imagination in the same way that Martin did with the Latin Explosion. Furthermore, Selena was coded as Chicana or Tejana not Latina.

Let me be clear in saying that I am not arguing that the term Latino is itself a new construction. It has been used in various ways and by various communities for some time. However, I am interested in charting the capitalist appropriation of the term Latino since the Latin Explosion and self-described Latina/os' use of the term in this space and time. For example, after this discourse we saw more Latina/o musicians in various manifestations, such as Shakira moving from Spanish-language to English-language music, the newly christened Latina Christina Aguilera moving from English- to Spanish-language music, and Mariah Carey becoming a cover girl for *Latina Magazine* twice. We also saw the rise of increasingly Latina/o marketed products such as the 2003 film *Chasing Papi*, billed as "the first major studio comedy to reflect the Hispanic cultural experience in America" ("About the Film"). As Shane Moreman and I have noted in our critique of the film, Latino comes to mean an undifferentiated identity that borrows signs, myths, and archetypes across groups as points of mutual identification, the conflation of Latino with Latin American, and the reification of stereotypes as a way to create "authentic Latino" identity. Products such as these differed from previous ethnic- and nationality-specific products geared toward Mexicans, Puerto Ricans, Cubans, and so on. This monolithic Latino identity suddenly became a new market that seemed to celebrate and revel in the fetish of difference that previous mainstream constructions such as Hispanic did not. Once again, the popular understandings of Latina/o identities had shifted. However, what was not so new, Valdivia argues, is that in these constructions "Latinas who can border cross traditional ethnic lines are more likely to be favored in representations within the mainstream" (13) and "Blackness once more gets pushed to the (left) margin" (15).

Describing the troubling use of the construction within the Latin music boom, Francis Aparicio writes, "The term Latin music boom deflects the social, demographic, and cultural realities of everyday life among U.S. Latinos and replaces what is socially real Latino with historically familiar, acceptable, and contained images of Latinos that the U.S. can integrate into its own logic" (91–92). Furthermore, scholars argue that the popular construction Latino can in effect erase differences between various Latina/o groups and create the illusion of a generic identity similar to the homogenization within the term Hispanic. Likewise, Mark Zimmerman is concerned with issues of power that relate to a generic Latino identity in that discourses within the United States equate Latino with Puerto Rican at the cost of other groups' identities and differences. Arlene Dávila, author of the book *Latinos Inc.*, noting the lack of complex Latina and Latino images, writes,

> in contrast to "women" or "teenagers" who are simultaneously segmented according to lifestyle, age, tastes, or race. "Hispanics" remain a protected segment by their mere definition as a homogeneously bounded, "culturally defined" niche. It is this defini-tion, which makes all "Latinos" part of the same undifferentiated "market"—whether they live in El Barrio or in an upscale New York high-rise ... (8)

Adding to this discussion, Alicia Gaspar de Alba notes, "We must examine at what point their respective differences align within each one's identity wheel, so that, rather than subsuming Chicana under Latina—or umbilically connecting them under the 'broader,' more hegemonic or homogenizing term, we are pulling them apart and seeing how they work together" (109). In the construction of these popular Latino images and representations, Dávila argues that U.S.-born Latinas and Latinos are presented as foreign or Latin American rather than as U.S.-based. Furthermore, advertisers view these foreign images as more ethnically "authentic" than images that address Latina/os as U.S.-born or acculturated (Dávila 69). Through these tactics U.S. Latina/os are thus rendered invisible, and histories of injustice are all but ignored.

I echo both Dávila and Gaspar de Alba's concern, having written about my own experiences in central New York working against anti-Mexican advertising.[3] My students' and my concerns that these ads were offensive were dismissed initially by executives at the company that produced them;

I was told that Latinos who worked for the company did not find the content objectionable. These Latinos, I explained, who were most likely Puerto Ricans or Dominicans, would not necessarily find these ads offensive as they were not the butt of the joke. The adoption of a monolithic Latina/o consuming body by advertisers and companies is irresponsible and dangerous in cases such as this. The point then becomes for those of us who are concerned with constructing a "Latina/o" identification to work toward creating images or representations that are not reductionist, representations that allow for some connection without homogeneity. In working toward this goal, however, I am sensitive to the ways that potential organizing terms such as women or Latinos can be simplistic, historically reductionist, and "ineffectual in designing strategies to combat oppressions" (Mohanty 31), as they often simply serve to reinforce binaries. Mohanty cautions, "Strategic coalitions that construct oppositional political identities for themselves are based on generalization and provisional unities, but the analysis of these group identities cannot be based on universalistic, ahistorical categories" (37).

Against the capitalist creation of a homogenized generic Latino identity and with the motivation of political unity, scholars are beginning to theorize ways to bridge differences across Latina/o groups. As the transnational flow of Latina/os continues, as we move into spaces beyond those traditionally associated with Latina/o communities such as the South, and as various Latina/o groups encounter each other in ways that they have not previously, finding points of connection becomes increasingly important. Thus, scholars of Latina/o studies have begun to explore the possibilities of performances of what has been termed *latinidad* that are based on affective connections rather than on more typical identification markers. For example, Francis Aparicio defines *latinidad* "as a concept that allows us to explore moments of convergences and divergences in the formation of Latino/a (post)colonial subjectivities and in hybrid cultural expressions among various Latino national groups" (93). *Latinidad* manifested in cultural texts "evokes in its audience, and perhaps to its interpreter, an analogous structure of feeling having to with the pain of exile and of geocultural displacements" (Aparicio 93). Similarly, José Esteban Muñoz sees *latinidad* as "an anti-normative affect" that "engenders a model of group identity that is not exclusionary, yet still coherent" ("Memory Performance" 100). Muñoz elaborates on this idea when he writes of "feeling brown" as a way to describe an affect of Otherness shared by Latina/os, whose affect is "often off" in comparison to what is constructed as normative national affect. He argues that the affect of Latina/os is often seen as inappropriate, as it does not match the official national affect associated with white middle-class subjectivities.

Finding a space to articulate pan-Latina/o identities or *latinidad* is not an easy task. Finding spaces that honor unity without erasing difference is difficult when you have communities as heterogeneous as those that fall under the umbrella term Latina/o. Furthermore, past attempts even at nationality-based movements have failed because of their lack of reflexivity when it comes to issues of sexuality and gender. Up-and-coming scholars such as Lisa Calvente have begun to address questions of affect and community that bring Latina/os into the fold by working through Gilroy's discussion of the Black Atlantic and hip-hop. Similarly, Raquel Rivera has written the long-silenced history of Latina/os in the formation of hip-hop. While these projects are not necessarily working through issues of pan-Latina/o identity, I find their approaches to affect, community, and the African diaspora to be of central importance as they work to challenge the black and white dichotomy that continues falsely to govern Latina/o identities. In taking a cue from these scholars, I turn to hip-hop and Reggaeton to make some preliminary gestures toward what I believe to be moment of possibility for *latinidad*.

"We're Latinos, Not Latino Rappers"

On September 7, 2000, the hip-hop world mourned the death of Christopher Rios, more commonly known to his fans as Big Pun or Big Punisher. Sadly, at the age of 28, Pun died of a heart attack and respiratory failure. Pun, a former model, had reached a level of morbid obesity that he was fighting at the time of his death. He, unlike many other Latino rappers, such as Kid Frost, Lighter Shade of Brown, and Proper Dos, had reached a level of national success and prominence; others tended to be regionally segmented.[4] In examining Chicano rap, Delgado argues that nationalist themes and re-articulation of Chicano politics are central ("Chicano Ideology"; "All Along the Border"). These themes, while unifying for Chicana/o listeners, have the potential to alienate non-Chicana/o listeners. Of these artists and their reception in hip-hop, Raquel Rivera, author of *New York Ricans in the Hip Hop Zone*, argues that the rappers who worked with

> explicitly Latino themes, language and/or sources in their music, often were shunned—
> by African Americans and Latinos alike—for stepping out of the hip hop norm. While

brief or peripheral Latino references and influences have been deemed acceptable, it seems as if there has been an 'insider' cutoff point on acceptability—shifting and highly subjective, but nonetheless real. (152)

This history and reception seemed to weigh heavily on artists such as Pun, whom Rivera quotes as saying, "What makes us special is that we're Latino, not Latino rappers. We mastered Black music—Hip Hop—not the Latino style of hip hop" (154). This approach and the fact that Pun's rise to fame coincided with the "Latin Explosion" in pop music contributed to his success.

Furthermore, the influence of the Latin Explosion in hip-hop could also be seen in changes in music and in the move by more African American rappers to incorporate Spanish or Latina/o themes into their music. Discussing this trend, Rivera argues that it is "easier an African American rapper to use cultural elements readily identifiable with Latinos than it is for Latinos themselves to do so" (193). Rivera quotes La Bruja, who argues "'Lil' Kim can say something in Spanish and everyone thinks it's crazy cool; but a Latino that tries that to use his or her culture and mix it in. … That hypothetical Latino runs the risk of being accused of overemphasizing and pimping his or her ethnicity and shunned for turning his or her back on 'true' hip hop" (193). Post-Pun and after the Latin Explosion it could be argued that this trend shifted *just a bit* with the increasing popularity of artists in hip-hop such as Fat Joe and N.O.R.E. and later the emergence of Reggaeton.

Bronx-born Pun was in no way shy about his Puerto Rican identity, as he was often draped in clothes featuring the Puerto Rican flag. Along with others in his clique, the Terror Squad, including fellow Puerto Rican Fat Joe, he represented not only urban Puerto Ricans or Boricuas through hits such as "100%" and "Still Not a Player," but also gave visibility to Spanish, Spanglish and urban Latina/o identifications. For example, the video for the single "100%" begins with airline attendant "Iris Chacón" announcing that the plane is close to reaching San Juan, Puerto Rico. Chacón was a famous Puerto Rican dancer/singer/entertainer. Another example of Pun's taking into account a Latina/o affect occurs in the video for "It's So Hard," which begins with people across the globe listening to Pun; simultaneously, celebrities such as Jennifer Lopez (whom Pun appeared with in a song), N.O.R.E., and Fat Joe pay homage to the deceased rapper. Though Pun released only three albums (some were released posthumously), *Capital Punishment*, *Yeeeah Baby*, and *Endangered Species*, his legacy in hip-hop and, specifically, in the emergence and acceptance of Reggaeton by mainstream audiences remains immeasurable. I, as well as Rivera, argue that the emergence of the discourse or construction of Latino as Pun reached stardom during the Latin Explosion created a space for artists such as Big Pun to emerge and "cross over," which previous Latina/o artists could not do. These spaces enabled new identifications and points of solidarity across difference.

In these highly visible mainstream spaces, Latino became a discourse that had the ability to homogenize or create spaces of unity. Echoing Aparico's discussion of *latinidad* as a point of shared feeling and convergence among Latina/o groups, I see the narratives, spaces, and affects offered by Pun and his later contemporaries such as N.O.R.E. and Don Omar creating these spaces, whether it be through performing biculturalism, explicitly claiming a Pan-Latina/o identity, or through narratives that attest to struggle. Writing of the affective quality of music, DeChaine argues,

> Affect is thus the circuit through which the past and present, as well as imaginings of the future, become confluent. It enables the process of becoming, entangling our bodies, minds, memories, histories, thoughts, and feelings to the point where they can't be imagined apart from each other ... I describe affect as an amplifier for the "music" of poetic language. Thus, conceived, affect gives us a way to understand how thoughts feel and how feelings think. Perhaps one of the reasons it is so difficult to talk about affect or designate it as a coherent form of knowledge is that, by and large, we don't really have a way to signify something that doesn't signify *per se*. Our words fail us. (86)

These songs and their stories act as affective spaces that recuperate the term Latino (at times an identity fraught with ambivalence) by creating spaces of convergence and affective identification for Latina/os on the basis of the possibility or reinscribing Latina/o as a site that creates unity while maintaining difference. They can operate in ways similar to Gilroy's "Black Atlantic," providing a shared structure of feeling.

As argued by Madison, the performed personal narrative implicates the audience, spurs it into action, as it is a "voice wedded to experience" ("Performance, Personal Narrative" 278). In the space of the music, of the performance, "listeners ... are ... affected by what they see and hear in ways that motivate them to act/think in forms that now beneficially affect (directly or indirectly) either the Subjects themselves or what they advocate" (280). Kim Purnell, in her study of Billie Holiday's music as personal narrative, makes a similar claim about the possibility of personal narrative to implicate community and challenge master narratives. As DeChaine writes of the affective possibility of music in community building, "the liminal character of musical experience, bodies coming together in spontaneous communitas, the promise and risk both individual and social transformation, aided and abetted by the consciousness participants share and the spaces they inhabit" (82). Keeping in mind this work I want to consider briefly the potentialities of identities performed and offered in Reggaeton.

The Chosen Few

Considering the possibility of music to actualize spaces of pan-Latina/o identity or *latinidad*, I make some preliminary gestures toward Reggaeton, which I see as part of Pun's legacy because of the emergence of some of his contemporaries and because I feel he opened up a space for Latina/os in urban popular music. Specifically, I am interested in N.O.R.E.'s "Oye Mi Canto" (feat. Nina Sky, Gem Star, Daddy Yankee, and Big Mato), considered the breakthrough hit that introduced Reggaeton to mainstream U.S. audiences (Jones). Of the song, Reggaeton star Daddy Yankee remarks, "That song Oye Mi Canto was the key to introducing reggaeton to the masses. ... It's like what Rapper's Delight (by the Sugarhill Gang) was for the hip-hop movement of the early '80s" (Jones). I also turn to Don Omar's "Reggaeton Latino Remix" (feat. N.O.R.E., Fat Joe, and LDA), because like "Oye Mi Canto" it was one of the first crossover hits and it featured a combination of different artists. My interest in these songs is not to exclude a long history of other Reggaeton artists; both songs maximize their crossover appeal because they include English, which is appealing not only to non-Spanish speakers but specifically to those Latina/os who are not bilingual, and because they are perhaps among the best-known to audiences not immediately familiar with the world of Reggaeton.

Reggaeton is a musical genre connected to Panama in the 1970s and Jamaicans whose ancestors had helped build the Panama Canal (Jones). The documentary *The Chosen Few* ties the origins of Reggaeton to Panama and the performer El General, who wanted to make reggae music in Spanish, which eventually morphed into Reggaeton. The music also became popular in Puerto Rico, where it really took off (*The Chosen Few*). Since the music broke through into the U.S. mainstream in 2004 with N.O.R.E.'s hit, Reggaeton artists have sold well over a million records (Andrade) and have been signed to work with major records labels such as Bad Boy and Universal Music Latino/ Machete Music. Former music producer Toy Hernandez attributes the success of Reggaeton to Latina/o buying power and the machinations of urban Latino culture: "[Latinos] are living in a different way, incorporating the hip-hop lifestyle the same way black and white communities have incorporated it in the past ... to me it is the same thing that happened 30 years ago with salsa and 15 years ago with pop music" (as qtd. in Andrade 52). Elaborating on the success of the genre, Daddy Yankee states, "No other music can [do] or ever [has done] what we are doing right now. We are [reaching] Mexicans, Dominicans, Colombians, Puerto Ricans, everybody because it's the first time that we speak for the urban people out there in the streets, everyday people" (Cepeda "Americano Idols" 117). While Reggaeton music is clearly breaking down boundaries and creating community for Latina/os, sexist and heterosexist aspects and the objectification of women do remain staples. However, it seems as if more women are working their way up the ranks.

N.O.R.E.'s "Oye Mi Canto," considered the song that broke Reggaeton wide open for mainstream audiences, offers a vision of Latino that defies national/ethnic differences while using the term to serve as a point of identification. Of the song and his desire to bring Reggaeton to a national level, N.O.R.E. comments,

> Reggaeton is in my blood like hip-hop because I am half Latino-American. ... I fell in love with this music. I did this joint originally as a mixtape. The Latino people haven't been spoken to in a while, since (Big) Pun died. They haven't felt like they had something proud [in hip-hop] to stand on, so being both Latin and black, I wanted to rep my Latin side for once. Why not do it with this new music, instead of doing a Spanish rap record? This is what speaks for the inner-city Latino youth. (Hall "N.O.R.E. Reps")

N.O.R.E.'s vision of a space for Latina/o people to have a sense of pride certainly comes through in the song and the video, though it really is a Latino identification and not necessarily Latina-friendly. N.O.R.E.'s anthem begins by asking all Latinos who are proud of their heritage to stand up as Nina Sky, a duo of Puerto Rican twin sisters, reference various Latino nationalities. In the video for the song, Latinas in bikinis carry and dance around the flags of their respective countries/cultures as N.O.R.E. and the other men walk among them wearing shirts that feature all of the flags. Cameras scale the women's bodies as if they are props of nationality (an interesting trope as women are often conflated with the nation). Soon the song moves from being simply an anthem of Latino pride toward being a song about "slapping *culo*" (slapping ass) as the lyrics mirror the tone of the video. In the video other Latino stars aside from the artists featured in the track, such as Fat Joe and Cuban rapper Pitbull, appear. Ending the track, N.O.R.E. exclaims that regardless of your race, "today you're Latino!" reinforcing his vision of a Latino nation that has the ability to unify across difference, putting aside individual agendas for a greater cause. He finishes by giving shout-outs including one to Pun at the end of the song.

While N.O.R.E.'s anthem potentially has the power to interpellate multiple Latina/o listeners through its catchy rhymes and its desire for a pan-Latina/o identification that does not compromise cultural specificity, the overwhelming maleness of the track and video is undeniable. Don Omar's "Reggaeton Latino Remix" continues the move toward a united Latina/o nation. The song begins with some macho posturing by N.O.R.E. and Fat Joe, who respectively name themselves as Latinos who are Ecuadorian, Panamanian, Nicaraguan, and Boricua. U.S.-born Fat Joe and N.O.R.E., together with Puerto Rican native Don Omar, collaborate on a track that brings together primarily Spanish-speaking artists with artists who have a very different relationship with Spanish, such as Joe, who admits his lack of fluency in Spanish. The bringing together of these two different perspectives in terms of generation/migration and language differences is significant in creating a united or pan-Latina/o space, particularly because of the authenticity games that often emerge in pan-Latina/o movements, as well as moving Latina/o from a U.S.-centered identity formation.

As the video for the song progresses, images of Che Guevara, Rita Moreno, César Chavez, Roberto Clemente, Tito Puente, Frida Kahlo, Diego Rivera, Big Pun, and other Latino luminaries flash across the screen along with multiple flags. Thus, the video extols Latina/o perseverance and struggle as spaces of identification and pride regardless of national origin or ethnicity, as well as U.S.-based or Latin-American-based differentials. However, it is the female performer, LDA, who delivers the most potent verse in the song, perhaps feeding into the ideology of women as being associated with nationhood. She names Latina/os as being the "cosmic race" or universal people. This verse also references Spain, South America, the United States, and Central America, all within the united Latina/o nation, a nation that crosses borders and boundaries much like a diaspora; in this case, however, peoples are linked together by a history of colonialism and struggle that has made them stronger. The verse is followed with a verse which roughly translates as Latina/os are the chosen few who are responsible for maintaining a united Latino nation. Present in this song and in the documentary *The Chosen Few*, the theme of the "chosen people" or "chosen few" almost takes on a mythic or religious aspect in the song.

The lyrics and the images cast Latina/os as survivors, able to work through adversity, and in a sense stronger because of the multiplicity of differences behind Latina/o. Don Omar comments on the presentation of a Latino identity:

> I'm so proud to be Latino. ... I'm so proud. We've got people in Latin America—Venezuelans, Colombians, Nicaraguans, Ecuadorians. When we made "Reggaeton Latino," we never expected that it's gonna be so big. That's a moment that all Latinos forget about where you are. No, I'm Latino. Forget about if you're from PR, forget about if you are from Cuba. We are Latinos. And I think "Reggaeton Latino" broke the rules. (Reid)

Don Omar speaks of an affective space that allows people temporarily to displace their senses of nationalism and difference for a greater Latina/o good. Through the music listeners are interpellated to think beyond or across nationalist and ethnic boundaries as a way to enact and perform political possibilities not previously available.

In thinking through what I like to consider spaces of possibility that exist in Reggaeton, I in no way want to downplay the masculine or heterosexual biases of the spaces or the fact that these are not necessarily altruistic spaces, that they are very much commodities. As discussed in the examples presented earlier, Reggaeton can be space where, as in much of popular culture, women's bodies rather than their voices or perspectives are front and center. For example, in describing the role sex plays in Reggaeton, the majority of the male artists featured in *The Chosen Few* connect the music to the movement of women's bodies and the possibility of sex. Commenting on this, female artist La Bruja describes the way that women's bodies are front and center in the music and imagery and jokes about reversing the image by putting men's bodies on display in her next video (*The Chosen Few*). Furthermore, performer Mala Rodriguez describes the music as more party focused, "less transcendental," more commercial than Latin hip-hop (*The Chosen Few*). Speaking of the possibility of women making space for themselves in Reggaeton, artists such as Glory describe the "macho man attitude in the genre," while Valery shares, "It's a man's world you know what you get yourself into" (*The Chosen Few*). Thus, it seems that Reggaeton can be space where women are objectified in the music and have to work twice as hard as artists to be considered something other than sex objects.

Of a similar situation in hip-hop Patricia Hill Collins raises the question "Quite simply, for Black women and other women of color, is there much space for the fusion of feminism (loving ourselves) and nationalism (race loyalty)?" (*From Black Power to Hip Hop* 161). Scholars such as Gwen Pough argue that such a space exists, while Hill Collins ties the possibility of feminism for the hip-hop generation to the politics of third-wave feminism and the remaking of the slogan "The Personal Is Political" (*From Black Power to Hip Hop*). Hill Collins argues that these women "do manage to find feminism increasingly carve out a space that simultaneously accepts and rejects the tenents of feminism and nationalism" (*From Black Power to Hip Hop* 162). Third-wave feminists embrace contradiction and tend to see change and issues of justice on a personal or everyday level rather than the more typical large-scale movement embraced by their predecessors (*From Black Power to Hip Hop*). Hill Collins argues that for the hip-hop generation, "women's movement mobilization occurs not within bureaucracies of the state or higher education but within popular culture and mass media" (*From Black Power to Hip Hop* 191). I turn to Hill Collins because even though she is writing about hip-hop, I believe the issues she raises for women of color in the hip-hop generation apply equally well to women performers of and listeners to Reggaeton who are interpellated by the music, which can reinforce their ethnic and national identities while simultaneously negating their identities as women. It's a complex negotiation that takes place and may not work for everyone; however, it is important to consider the ways that a third-wave feminist perspective that embraces contradiction or a hip-hop feminist perspective that has redefined the slogan "The Personal Is Political" makes this more complex than a simple case of saying that Reggaeton is sexist and women are excluded. For example, Reggaeton personalities, both male and female, have been consistently presented in the pages of *Latina* since its emergence.

In addition, it is important to discuss the fact that in this case identity is also a commodity, something about which the artists speak freely. Arguing about the emergence of Reggaeton in the mainstream, artist Pitbull states that Latina/os now have demographic numbers that make them the majority in the United States and it makes sense (*The Chosen Few*). He argues that Latina/os are now the majority and that we must "take advantage of the opportunity" (*The Chosen Few*). This same attitude is expressed by Fat Joe, who argues that Latina/os need to support the artists by buying their albums (*The Chosen Few*). I am not naïve enough to believe that the artists are simply in this to create a reclaimed sense of identity; clearly capitalism plays an extremely large part in the ways these identities are shaped and presented. However, I believe it is important to chart what an already commodified identity such as Latina/o means when Latina/os themselves adopt the term for their own uses, particularly when they work within the realm of commodity as well. How does this term become imbued with possibility and subversive politics? It can be likened to Delgado's argument regarding vernacular uses of the term Hispanic versus dominant assimilationist constructions ("When the Silenced Speak"). How do these discourses differ from other Latino constructions such as those presented in the 2003 film *Chasing Papi*, in which Latino exists as a monolithic undifferentiated identity (Calafell and Moreman)? Scholars have argued for the popular culture to be a site of possibility and community building despite its capitalist functions (Calafell and Delgado), but Hill Collins raises an important issue: "This new version of personal politics expressed within popular culture venues is important, but representations that remain untethered to actual social movements make it difficult for popular-culture consumers to tell whether they are participating in an important new form of feminist politics or merely being entertained by it" (*From Black Power to Hip Hop* 193). In the end Hill Collins and others argue for the possibility of these sites. Even recently I reflected on how listening to Chicano rap in my youth had the lasting effect of instilling Chicano nationalism or cultural pride that I did not necessarily receive at home and how my home experiences contributed to a Chicana feminist perspective.

I do not assume that Reggaeton will change the world. I do not even know or attempt to make a guess about how long the genre will last or what it will become; rather, I see the value in some of the present conversation about Latina/o as a space for identification that asks us to momentarily displace our nationalist tendencies for a larger, more global identification. In this displacement we are not asked to ignore or gloss over our individual histories (both personal and culturally social); rather, we are asked to consider how these histories enable spaces of identification with Others who share an affect of Otherness based on factors such as language and colonialism. We can understand that art can be political, and Boal, speaking of theater, saw it as a rehearsal for the revolution. In the same way I want to consider the ways that Reggaeton offers Latina/o as something more than what it has been in the past, an identity that calls for unity while maintaining some semblance of difference. Yes, it still exists in the realm of commodity, but does this foreclose all of its potential use value? When asked about the legacy of Reggaeton and how he would like to be remembered, Daddy Yankee shares that he wants people to say, "This guy did big things for his people, big things for Latinos" (*The Chosen Few*). In the same way, we can ask what can Reggaeton do for Latina/os?

· 7 ·

FINAL THOUGHTS

In this text I have attempted to map some of the terrain of Latina/o performance in the field of communication studies by examining performance from a variety of perspectives. I have moved from the study of performances of identity and community in everyday life to the study of performance as it intersects with popular culture. These choices reflect my desire to get us to consider how each of us engages in or engages with performance in multiple ways and contexts. In my approach to these subjects I have also attempted to model or utilize a variety of methodological tools ranging from autobiographical performance to performance ethnography and textual analysis. Each of these choices is centered in my desire to open up the ways we understand the study of performance in the field. Again, this project has been about situating performance not necessarily on a formal stage but on the stage we call our lives. At the beginning of this text I outlined a trajectory for Latina/o performance in communication studies, and it was quite small. My hope is that this book serves as an invitation for others to begin to have conversations about Latina/o performance that forces performance studies to see the importance of these communities and recognize what we can learn from them about performance.

Among my fundamental desires in writing this text has also been to challenge the largely oppressive black and white dichotomy that continues to reign in mainstream discussions of race and ethnicity and in the pages of our professional journals, where Latina/os, Native Americans, and Asian Americans are virtually nonexistent. Through engagement with texts such as Ricky Martin or Reggaeton, I hope to have demonstrated some of the contours that guide Latina/o identities in ways that often defy dominant logics of race and ethnicity. As Latina/os continue to be the largest "minority" group in the country, can we really hold on to our simplistic understandings of race? Can we continue to deny the existence of mixed-raced identities and the everyday reverberations of colonialism? It is my hope that this text contributes to a more nuanced understanding of race and ethnicity and attests to the importance of Latina/o studies in the field of communication.

Another central tenet with which I begin this book is that identity matters. Identity matters as an object of study, as a process, and for us as researchers. While I am sure many would agree with this statement, I feel it is important to restate and defend my stand because of the constant onslaught of charges of narcissism leveled against scholars in performance, particularly scholars of color, who must often justify the importance of their voices and texts in ways that white scholars are neither expected nor required to. I am reminded of the words of my dear mentor and friend Fernando Delgado, who writes of his own frustrations as a rhetorical critic:

> As a rhetorician raised as a Mexican American, I nevertheless have had to read Conwell, understand the Grange Movement, and examine liberalism because they are deemed fundamentally American discourses. What I ask why is it so hard for others to understand that Chavez, the American Indian Movement, and Afrocentricity are no less American? Should mainstream ignorance always be related to questioning minority legitimacy? ("The Dilemma of the Minority Scholar" 51)

I feel Delgado's frustration because it is my own. I hope this text can serve as a challenge to these types of logics, which in many cases govern our field and specifically our journals. For example, even though I was hired to teach rhetoric in my first faculty appointment, I soon learned that it was all a farce. I would always be reminded in both subtle and not so subtle ways that I was not really considered a part of the rhetoric concentration, as if somehow my critical orientation was not in line with the "criticism" in rhetorical criticism—illustrating to me that while minority bodies are desired, minority perspectives are not.

Returning to the discussion of the importance of identity, like Gingrich-Philbrook and Madison ("The Dialogic Performative") I am also concerned with trends in autoethnography. They point to issues of poetics and the lack of dialogue that can sometimes occur; I agree with them and am interested in the ways that autoethnography, a tool initially conceived as a way for Others to talk back or bring their subjectivities to bear on research, has seemed to obscure the voices of people of color while centering the narratives of white women academics (e.g., narratives of white female academics during 9/11 negotiating their fear of the Other/taxi driver). I keep in mind Paula Moya's words that "some identities can be more politically progressive than others, *not* because they are 'transgressive' or 'indeterminate' but because they provide us with a critical perspective from which we can disclose the complicated workings of ideology and oppression" (27). Writing of the project of autoethnography, performance scholar Stacey Holman Jones argues, "Autoethnographic texts focus on how subordinated people use deliberately subtle and opaque forms of communication—forms that are not textual or visual—to express their thoughts, feelings, and desires by performing these practices on the page and on the stage" (767). Holman Jones narrates a hopeful project that connects voices to bodies that are wedded to experience and performances that are potentially decolonial. However, this is a best-case scenario. The hope that the embodied telling of story will spur an audience or reader into action, "centered on the principles of transformation and transgression, dialogue and interrogation"—what Madison calls a performance of possibilities—is lost as apolitical, narcissistic, and ironically unreflexive work continues to dominate ("Performance, Personal Narratives" 278). Women of color scholars, such as Moraga and Anzaldúa, whose work embodies the political goals of autoethnography, the desire to center our stories, who have long argued for making connections between collective, cultural, and personal experiences, are completely ignored. Furthermore, I do not assume that the work I have presented here that engages the personal is exemplary or without scope for critique, but it has been my conscious effort in engaging in such work to consider the ways my voice can move beyond myself to shed some light on the larger historical and social factors in my cultures. This has been also been a guiding force in the writing of this text.

While I have offered some final thoughts about Latina/o performance, there remains a great deal more work to be done, particularly in relation to issues of pan-Latina/o identity, migration patterns, immigration, and transnationalism. I hope this text can serve as a conversation opener.

NOTES

Chapter 2

Copyright 2004 from "Disrupting the Dichotomy?: 'Yo Soy Chicana/o?' in the New Latina/o South" published in *The Communication Review* by Bernadette Marie Calafell. Reproduced by permission of Taylor and Francis Group, LLC, http://www.taylorandfrancis.com.

1. I do not assume this is the case in every Southwestern city, particularly those small or possibly rural towns, but generally the Southwest because of its history and proximity to the Mexican border feels more like "home" in some ways than the Southeast.
2. National Association for Chicana and Chicano Studies.

Chapter 3

Copyright 2005 from "Pro(re-)claiming Loss: A Performative Pilgrimage in Search of Malintzin Tenépal" published in *Text and Performance Quarterly* by Bernadette Marie Calafell. Reproduced by permission of Taylor and Francis Group, LLC, http://www.taylorandfrancis.com.

1. Refers to Cherrie Moraga, specifically her poem "La Dulce Culpa."
2. Juan Jarmillo was the solider Cortés married Malintzin off to when his Spanish wife came to Mexico.

Chapter 4

1. After these documentaries, El Vez appeared in more popular forums such as advertisements for the cable network USA.

Chapter 5

The author thanks Tes Thraves for use of the photograph at the end of this chapter.

1. Thomas K. Nakayama. "Show/down Time: 'Race,' Gender, Sexuality, and Popular Culture." *Critical Studies in Mass Communication* 8 (1994): 162–179.

Chapter 6

1. Some prominent examples of this discussion include Francis Aparicio's "Jennifer As Selena: Rethinking Latinidad in Media and Popular Culture." *Latino Studies* 1 (2003): 90–105; Alicia Gaspar de Alba's "The Chicana/Latina Dyad, or Identity and Perception." *Latino Studies* 1 (2003): 106–114; Angharad Valdivia's "Latinas As Radical Hybrid: Transnationally Gendered Traces in Mainstream Media." *Global Media Journal* (2004): 1–21; and Marc Zimmerman's "Erasure, Imposition and Crossover of Puerto Ricans and Chicanos in US Film and Music Culture." *Latino Studies* 1 (2003): 115–122.

2. See Bernadette Marie Calafell and Fernando Delgado. "Reading Latina/o Images: Interrogating Americanos." *Critical Studies in Media Communication* 21 (2004): 1–21; and Bernadette Marie Calafell. "Disrupting the Dichotomy: 'Yo Soy Chicana/o?' in the New Latina/o South." *Communication Review* 7 (2004): 175–204 or chapter 2 in this volume.

3. Bernadette Marie Calafell. "Mocking Mexicans for Profit." *Latino Studies* 4 (2006): 162–165.

4. This is not to discount the unrecognized history of Puerto Ricans in the evolution of hip-hop, which Raquel Rivera recounts in *New York Ricans in the Hip Hop Zone*; rather, it is central to understanding the visibility Pun received as a Latino.

WORKS CITED

"About the Film." *Chasing Papi*, July 12, 2004; www.chasingpapi.com/about01.html.

Ahmed, Sara. *Strange Encounters: Embodied Others in Post-Coloniality*. London: Routledge, 2000.

Alarcón, Norma. "Conjugating Subjects in the Age of Multiculturalism." *Mapping Multiculturalism*. Eds. Avery F. Gordon and Christopher Newfield. Minneapolis, MN: U of Minnesota P, 1996. 127–148.

Alcoff, Linda Martín. "Latino/as, Asian Americans, and the Black–White Binary." *The Journal of Ethics* 7 (2003): 5–27.

———, and Satya P. Mohanty. "Reconsidering Identity Politics: An Introduction." *Identity Politics Reconsidered*. Eds. Linda Martín Alcoff, Michael Hames-García, Satya P. Mohanty, and Paula M.L. Moya. New York: Palgrave, 2006. 1–9.

———, Michael Hames-García, Satya P. Mohanty, and Paula M.L. Moya. Eds. *Identity Politics Reconsidered*. New York: Palgrave, 2006.

Altman, Dennis. "Rupture or Continuity? The Internationalization of Gay Identities." *Post-Colonial Queer: Theoretical Intersections*. Ed. John C. Hawley. Albany, NY: State U of New York, 2001. 19–41.

Alvarez, Julia. "A White Woman of Color." *Half and Half: Writers on Growing Up Biracial and Bicultural*. Ed. Claudine Chiawei O'Hearn. New York: Pantheon, 1998. 139–149.

Americanos: Latino Life in the United States. Home Box Office, 2000.

Andrade, Javier. "Mas Gasolina?" *Hispanic* May 2006: 50–54.

Anzaldúa, Gloria. *Borderlands/La Frontera: The New Mestiza*. San Francisco: Aunt Lute, 1987.

———. "Bridge, Drawbridge, Sandbar or Island: Lesbians-of-Color *Hacienda Alizanas*." *Bridges of Power: Women's Multicultural Alliances*. Eds. Lisa Albrecht and Rosa M. Brewer. Philadelphia: New Society, 1990. 216–231.

Anzaldúa Gloria. "Preface: Unatural Bridges, (Un)safe Spaces." *This Bridge We Call Home: Radical Visions for Transformation*. Eds. Gloria Anzaldúa and Ana Louise Keating. New York: Routledge, 2002. 1–5.

"AOL Chat." June 5, 1999. *Ricky Martin Official Homepage*. December 3, 1999; www. rickymartin.com/rickymartin/english/aol_chat.html.

Aparicio, Francis R. "Jennifer As Selena: Rethinking Latinidad in Media and Popular Culture." *Latino Studies* 1 (2003): 90–105.

Arrizon, Alicia. *Latina Performance: Transversing the Stage*. Bloomington, IN: U of Indiana P, 1999.

Arteaga, Alfred. *Chicano Politics: Heterotexts and Hybridities*. Cambridge, UK: Cambridge UP, 1997.

Barbara Walters 10 Most Fascinating People of 1999. ABC. December 1999.

Battaglia, Debbora. "On Practical Nostalgia: Self-Prospecting among Urban Trobrianders." *Rhetorics of Self-Making*. Ed. Debbora Battaglia. Berkeley: U of California P, 1995. 77–96.

Behar, Ruth. *The Vulnerable Observer: Anthropology That Breaks Your Heart*. Boston, MA: Beacon, 1996.

Bell, David, and Jon Binnie. *The Sexual Citizen: Queer Politics and Beyond*. Cambridge: Polity, 2000.

Beltrán, Mary. "The Hollywood Latina Body As Site of Social Struggle: Media Constructions of Stardom and Jennifer Lopez's Crossover Butt." *Quarterly Review of Film and Video* 19 (2002): 71–86.

Berlant, Lauren and Elizabeth Freeman. "Queer Nationality." *Radical Street Performance: An International Anthology*. Ed. Jan Cohen-Cruz. New York: Routledge, 1998. 133–142.

Bersani, Leo. "Is the Rectum a Grave?" *AIDS: Cultural Analysis, Cultural Activism*. Ed. Douglas Crimp. Cambridge, MA: MIT Press, 1989. 198–222.

"Best and Worst Dressed '99: Ricky Martin." *People Weekly* September 22, 1999: 98–99.

Bhabha, Homi K. *The Location of Culture*. New York: Routledge, 1994.

Blackwell, Judi. "Blue Suede Sombrero." *Metroactive Music* November 27, 1996. November 11, 2001; http://www.metroactive.com/papers/metro/11.27.96/el-vez-9648.html.

Blair, Carole. "Contemporary U.S. Memorial Sites As Exemplars of Rhetoric's Materiality." *Rhetorical Bodies*. Eds. Jack Selzer and Sharon Crowley. Madison: U of Wisconsin P, 1999. 16–57.

———, Marsha S. Jeppeson, and Enrico Pucci Jr. "Public Memorializing in Postmodernity: The Vietnam Veterans Memorial As Prototype." *Critical Questions: Invention, Creativity, and the Criticism of Discourse and Media*. Eds. William L. Nothstine, Carole Blair, and Gary A. Copeland. New York: St. Martin's, 1994. 350–382.

Boal, Augusto. *Theatre of the Oppressed*. Trans. Charles A. and Maria-Odilia Leal McBride. New York: Theatre Communications Group, 1985.

Bonim-Rodriguez, Paul. "Memory's Caretaker." *Text and Performance Quarterly* 24 (2004): 161–181.

Boym, Sveltlana. "On Diasporic Intimacy: Ilya Kabakov's Installations and Immigrants Homes." *Intimacy*. Ed. Lauren Berlant. Chicago, IL: U of Chicago P, 2000. 226–252.

Browne, David. "Boys to Men." *Entertainment Weekly Online* May 11, 1999. March 2, 2000; www.ew.com/ew/article/0,,64024,00.html.

Burke, Kenneth. *Rhetoric of Motives*. Berkeley: U of California P, 1969.

Cagle, Jess. "The Entertainers 99: Ricky Martin." *Entertainment Weekly Online* December 24, 1999. March 2, 2000; www.ew.com/ew/article/0,272182,00.html.

Caistor, Nick. *Cities of the Imagination: Mexico City*. New York: Interlink Books, 2000.

Calafell, Bernadette Marie. *More Than a Latin Lover: Ricky Martin and the Politics of Disidentification*. Unpublished Master's Thesis, Arizona State University, 2000.

———. "In Our Own Image? A Rhetorical Criticism of *Latina Magazine*." *Voces: A Journal of Chicana and Latina Studies* 3, 1/2 (2001): 12–46.

———. "Disrupting the Dichotomy: 'Yo Soy Chicana/o in the New Latina/o South." *The Communication Review* 7 (2004): 175–204.

———. "Pro(re-)claiming Loss: A Performative Pilgrimage in Search of Malintzin Tenépal." *Text and Performance Quarterly* 25 (2005): 43–56.

———. "Mocking Mexicans for Profit." *Latino Studies* 4 (2006): 162–165.

———. "Performing the Responsible Sponsor: Everything You Never Wanted to Know about Immigration Post-9/11." *Latina/o Communication Studies Today*. Ed. Angharad N. Valdivia. New York: Peter Lang, forthcoming.

———, and Fernando Delgado. "Reading Latina/o Images: Interrogating *Americanos*." *Critical Studies in Media Communication* 21 (2004): 1–21.

———, and Shane T. Moreman. "*Chasing Papi*, Chasing Authenticity: Creating the 'Latino' Film." Unpublished Manuscript, 2005.

Calvente, Lisa B. *The Black Atlantic Revisited: Nihilism, Matrices of Struggle and Hip Hop Culture*. Unpublished Master's Thesis, University of North Carolina, 2002.

———. "'Isn't This My Home Too?!' Between Latinidad and the Black Diaspora, A Puerto Rican's Story." Unpublished Conference Paper, Departures and Definitions of Afro-Latino and Afro-Latin American Identity in the New Millennium. New York, 2005.

Castillo, Ana. "The Distortion of Desire." *The Sexuality of Latinas*. Eds. Norma Alarcón, Ana Castillo, and Cherríe Moraga. Berkeley: Third World, 1993. 147–150.

Cepeda, María Elena. "*Mucho Loco* for Ricky Martin; Or the Politics of Chronology, Crossover, and Language within the Latin(o) Music 'Boom.'" *Popular Music and Society* 24 (2000): 51–71.

———. "'Columbus Effect(s)': Chronology and Crossover in the Latin(o) Music 'Boom.'" *Discourse* 23 (2001): 63–81.

———. "Shakira As the Idealized Transational Citizen: A Case Study of *Colombianidad* in Transition." *Latino Studies* 1 (2003): 211–232.

Cepeda, Raquel. "American Idols: Daddy Yankee." *Latina* March 2006: 116–118.

Chan, Sucheng. *Asian American: An Interpretative History*. Boston: Twayne, 1991.

Christian, Barbara. "The Race for Theory." *Making Face, Making Soul: Haciendo Caras*. Ed. Gloria Anzaldúa. San Francisco, CA: Aunt Lute, 1990. 335–345.

Christian, Karen. *Show and Tell: Identity As Performance in U.S. Latina/o Fiction*. Albuquerque: U of New Mexico P, 1997.

Cisneros, Sandra. *The House on Mango Street*. New York: Vintage, 1991.

Cohen-Cruz, Jan. Ed. *Radical Street Performance*. New York: Routledge. 1998.

Conquergood, Dwight. "Performing As a Moral Act: Ethical Dimensions of the Ethnography of Performance." *Literature in Performance: A Journal of Literary and Performing Art* 5 (1985): 1–13.

———. "Beyond the Text: Toward a Performative Cultural Politics." *The Future of Performance Studies: Visions and Revisions*. Ed. Sheron J. Dailey. Annandale, VA: National Communication Association, 1998. 25–36.

Cordova, Nathanial I. "The Constitutive Force of *Catecismo del Pueblo* in Puerto Rico's Popular Democratic Party Campaign of 1938–1940." *Quarterly Journal of Speech* 90 (2004): 212–233.

Corey, Frederick C. "The Personal: Against the Master Narrative." *The Future of Performance Studies: Visions and Revisions*. Ed. Sheron J. Dailey. Annandale, VA: National Communication Association, 1998. 249–253.

———. "On Possibility." *Text and Performance Quarterly* 26 (2006): 330–332.

Corpi, Lucha. "Marina." *Infinite Divisions: An Anthology of Chicana Literature*. Eds. Tey Diana Rebolledo and Eliana S. Rivero. Tucson, AZ: U of Arizona P, 1993. 196–197.

Cox, J. Robert. "Cultural Memory and Public Moral Argument." *The Van Zelst Lecture in Communication*. Northwestern University School of Speech. Evanston, Illinois. May 19, 1987.

———. "Memory. Critical Theory, and the Argument From History." *Argumentation and Advocacy* 27 (1990): 1–13.

Cruz, Mariolga Reyes. "*Mis Muertos Están Conmigo* (My Dead Are with Me)." *Qualitative Inquiry* 12 (2006): 589–595.

Cruz, Rene. *Omnibus Press Presents the Story of Ricky Martin*. London: Omnibus, 1999.

Dávila, Arlene. *Latinos Inc.: The Marketing and Making of a People*. Berkeley, CA: University of California Press, 2001.

Davis, Olga. "The Door of No Return: Reclaiming the Past Through the Rhetoric of Pilgrimage." *Western Journal of Black Studies* 21, 3 (1997): 156–162.

de Certeau, Michel. *The Practice of Everyday Life*. Trans. Steven Randell. Berkeley, CA: University of California, 1984.

DeChaine, D. Robert. "Affect and Embodied Understanding in Musical Experience." *Text and Performance Quarterly* 22 (2002): 79–98.

De La Garza, Sarah Amira. *María Speaks: Journeys into the Mysteries of the Mother in My Life As a Chicana*. New York: Peter Lang, 2004.

Del Castillo, Adelaida R. "Malinztín Tenépal: A Preliminary Look into a New Perspective." *Encuentro Femenil* 1/2 (1972): 58–77.

Delgado, Fernando Pedro. "Chicano Movement Rhetoric: An Ideographic Interpretation." *Communication Quarterly* 43 (1995): 446–455.

———. "The Dilemma of the Minority Scholar: Finding a Legitimized Voice in An Intellectual Space." *Proceedings of the National Communication Association 1997 Summer Conference: Racial and Ethnic Diversity in the 21st Century: A Communication Perspective*, July 24–27, 1999, Capital Hilton, Washington, D.C. Ed. Sherwyn P. Morreale. Annandale, VA: National Communication Association, 1997. 47–52.

———. "Chicano Ideology Revisited: Rap Music and the (Re)articulation of Chicanismo." *Western Journal of Communication* 62 (1998): 95–113.

———. "When the Silenced Speak. The Textualization and Complexities of Latino Identity." *Western Journal of Communication* 62 (1998): 420–438.

———. "The Rhetoric of Fidel Castro: Ideographs in the Service of Revolutionaries." *The Howard Journal of Communications* 10 (1999): 1–14.

———. "Rigoberta Menchú and Testimonial Discourse: The Integration of Collectivism and Rhetorical Criticism." *World Communication* 28 (1999): 17–29.

———. "All Along the Border: Kid Frost and the Performance of Brown Masculinity." *Text and Performance Quarterly* 20 (2000): 388–402.

———. "Golden But Not Brown: Oscar De La Hoya and the Complications of Culture, Manhood, and Boxing." *International Journal of the History of Sport* 22 (2005): 194–210.

———, and Bernadette Marie Calafell. "From Rico Suave to Livin' *La Vida Loca*: A Decade of Evolution for Latino Pop Star Images." *Race/Gender/Media: Considering Diversity Across*

Audiences, Content, and Producers. Ed. Rebecca Ann Lind. New York: Longman, 2004. 235–242.

Delgado, Celeste Fraser, and José Esteban Muñoz. Eds. "Rebellions of Everynight Life." *Everynight Life: Culture and Dance in Latin/o America.* Durham: Duke UP, 1991. 9–32.

Desmond, Jane C. "Embodying Difference: Issues in Dance and Cultural Studies." *Everynight Life: Culture and Dance in Latin/o America.* Eds. Celeste Fraser Delgado and José Esteban Muñoz. Durham: Duke UP, 1991. 33–64.

Di Leonardo, Micaela. *Exotics at Home: Anthropologies, Others, American Modernity.* U of Chicago, IL: Chicago P, 1998.

Diamond, Elin. Ed. "Introduction." *Performance and Cultural Politics.* New York: Routledge. 1–9.

Distribution of students by level, race, and sex, Fall 2000. *Office of Institutional Research fact book 2000–2001.* Retrieved January 11, 2004; http://www.ais.unc.edu/ir/fb0001/00table2.html.

Doxtader, Erik. "Making Rhetorical History in a Time of Transition: The Occasion, Constitution, and Representation of South African Reconciliation." *Rhetoric and Public Affairs* 4 (2001): 223–260.

———. "Reconciliation—A Rhetorical Concept/ion." *Quarterly Journal of Speech* 89 (2003): 267–292.

Drzewiecka, Jolanta A., & Rona T. Halualani. "The Structural–Cultural Dialectic of Diaspora Politics." *Communication Theory* 12, 3 (2002): 340–366.

Dyer, Richard. "Don't Look Now: The Instabilities of the Male Pin-up." *Only Entertainment.* London: Routledge, 1992. 103–119.

———. "Seen to Be Believed: Some Problems in the Representations of Gay People As Typical." *The Matter of Images: Essays on Representations.* London: Routledge, 1993. 19–51.

———. *White.* London: Routledge, 1997.

Edensor, Tim. "Walking, Gazing, Photographing and Remembering at the Taj." *Tourists at the Taj: Performance and Meaning at a Symbolic Site.* New York: Routledge, 1998. 105–148.

"*El Mundo* loves Ricky." *Time.com* March 2, 2000; http://www.time.com/time/daily/special/photo/martin/6.html.

El Rey de Rock n' Roll. Documentary. Dir. Marjorie Chodorov. Soap Box Films, 2000.

"El Vez Happening." December 5, 2001; http://www.cmp.ucr.edu/elvis/el_vez/el_vez.html.

Ellis, Carolyn. "Evocative Autoethnography: Writing Emotionally About Your Lives." *Representation and the Text: Reframing the Narrative Voice.* Eds. William Tierney and Yvonne. S. Lincoln. Albany: State of New York University P, 1997. 115–142.

———, and Arthur P. Bochner. "Autoethnograpy, Personal Narrative, Reflexivity: Researcher As Subject." *The Handbook of Qualitative Research (2nd ed.).* Eds. Norman K. Denzin and Yvonne S. Lincoln. Thousand Oaks, CA: Sage, 2000. 733–768.

Ellis, Robert Richmond. "Introduction." *Reading and Writing the Ambiente: Queer Sexualities in Latino, Latin American, and Spanish Culture.* Eds. Susana Chávez-Silverman and Librada Hernández. Madison, WI: U of Wisconsin P, 2000. 1–18.

Enck-Wanzer, Darrel. "Trashing the System: Social Movement, Interesectional Rhetoric, and Collective Agency in the Young Lords Organization's Garbage Offensive." *Quarterly Journal of Speech* 92 (2006): 174.

Essex, Andrew. "Not So Little Ricky." *Entertainment Weekly Online* April 23, 1999. March 2, 2000; www.ew.com/ew/article/0,,273151,00.html.

Esquire. January 2000: cover.

Ethnic & community development—Town of Carrboro. *Town of Carrboro, NC—est. 1911.* Retrieved January 11, 2004; http://www.ci.carrboro.nc.us/ECD/demographics.htm.

Fact sheet—American-Fact finder. *U.S. Census Bureau.* Retrieved January 7, 2004; http://factfinder.census.gov/home/en/epss/glossary_r.html#race.

Facts for features. *U.S. Census Bureau.* Retrieved January 12, 2004; http://www.census.gov/Press-Release/www/2003/cb03-ff14.htm.

Fanon, Frantz. *The Wretched of the Earth.* New York: Grove, 1963.

Farley, Christopher John. "Latin Music Pops." *Time* May 24, 1999: 74–79.

Feliciano, Melanie. "Ricky Martin in Concert: His Appeal Is Contagious." *Latinolink* November 26, 1999. December 8, 1999; http://www.latinolink.com/arts_entertainment/music/1126rick.htm.

Fernandez, Ruby Ann, and Richard J. Jensen. "Reies Lopez Tijerina's 'the Land Grant Question': Creating History Through Metaphors." *Howard Journal of Communications* 6 (1995): 129–145.

Flores, Lisa A. "Creating Discursive Space Through a Rhetoric of Difference: Chicana Feminists Craft a Homeland." *Quarterly Journal of Speech* 82 (1996): 142–156.

———. "Challening the Myth of Assimilation: A Chicana Feminist Response." *International and Intercultural Communication Annual Vol XXIII: Constituting Cultural Difference Through Discourse.* Ed. Mary Jane Collier. Thousand Oaks, CA: Sage, 2001. 26–46.

———. "Constructing Rhetorical Borders: Peons, Illegal Aliens, and Competing Narratives of Immigration." *Critical Studies in Media Communication* 20 (2003): 362–387.

———, and Hasian Marouf. "Returning to Aztlán and La Raza: Political Communication and the Vernacular Construction of Chicano/a Nationalism." *International and Intercultural Communication Annual Vol XX: Politics, Communication, and Culture.* Eds. Alberto González and Dolores V. Tanno. Thousand Oaks, CA: Sage, 1997. 186–203.

Foucault, Michel. "Sexual Choice, Sexual Act: Foucault and Homosexuality." *Politics, Philosophy, Culture: Interviews and Other Writings 1977–1984.* Trans. Alan Sheridan. Ed. Lawrence D. Kritzman. New York: Routledge, 1990. 286–303.

Friedan, Betty. "The Problem That Has No Name." *Social Theory: The Multicultural and Classical Readings.* Ed. Charles Lemert. Boulder, CO: Westview, 1999. 356–359.

Fusco, Coco. Ed. *Corpus Delecti: Performance Art of the Americas.* New York: Routledge, 2000.

Gaspar de Alba, Alicia. "The Chicana/Latina Dyad, or Identity and Perception." *Latino Studies* 1 (2003): 106–114.

Gilroy, Paul. *The Black Atlantic: Modernity and Double Consciousness.* Cambridge, MA: Harvard UP, 1993.

Gingrich-Philbrook, Craig. "Autoethnography's Family Values: Easy Access to Compulsory Experiences." *Text and Performance Quarterly* 25 (2005): 297–314.

Ginsberg, Elaine K. Ed. *Passing and the Fictions of Identity.* Durham: Duke, 1996.

Goffman, Erving. *The Presentation of Self in Everyday Life.* New York: Anchor, 1959.

Gómez-Peña, Guillermo. *The New World Border: Prophecies, Poems, and Loqueras For the End of the Century.* San Francisco, CA: City Lights, 1996.

González, Alberto. "Mexican 'Otherness' in the Rhetoric of Mexican Americans." *The Southern Communication Journal* 55 (1990): 276–291.

———, and Jennifer L. Willis-Rivera. "Remembering Selena." *Our Voices: Essays in Culture, Ethnicity, and Communication (4th ed).* Eds. Alberto González, Marsha Houston, and Victoria Chen. Los Angeles: Roxbury, 2004. 56–60.

Gonzalez, Carolina. "All That Glitters." *Frontera Magazine* December 6, 2001; http://www.fronteramag.com/issue4/features/elvez.htm.

Gonzalez, Jennifer. "Archeological Devotion." *With Other Eyes: Looking at Race and Gender in Visual Culture.* Ed. Lisa Bloom. Minneapolis: U of Minnesota P, 1999. 184–212.

Gonzalez, Maria Cristina. "The Four Seasons of Ethnography: A Creation Centered Ontology For Ethnography." *International Journal of Intercultural Relations* 24 (2000): 623–650.

2000 Grammy Awards. CBS

Griffiths, John. "Ricky Martin: Cross Appeal." *The National Advocate* July 6, 1999: 26–36.

Guillaumin, Colette. "The Constructed Body." *Reading the Social Body*. Trans. Diane Griffin Crowder. Eds. Catherine B. Burroughs and Jeffrey David Ehrenreich. Iowa City: U of Iowa P, 1993. 40–59.

Gutiérrez, David G. *Walls and Mirrors: Mexican Americans, Mexican Immigrants, and the Politics of Ethnicity* Berkeley, CA: University of California Press, 1995.

Habell-Pallán, Michelle. "El Vez Is 'Taking Care of Business': The Inter/National Appeal of Chicano Popular Music." *Cultural Studies* 13 (1999): 195–210.

———. *Loca Motion: The Travels of Latina Popular Culture*. New York: NYU Press, 2005.

Hall, Rashaun. "N.O.R.E. Reps His Latin Side With Reggaeton 'Oye Mi Canto'" *MTV News* November 3, 2004. Retrieved September 2, 2006 from www.mtv.com/news/articles/1493410/11032004/n_o_r_e_.jhtml.

Hall, Stuart. *Representation: Cultural Representations and Signifying Practices* (Culture, Media, and Identities, Vol 2). London: Sage, 1997.

Halperin, David. *Saint Foucault: Towards a Gay Hagiography*. New York: Oxford UP, 1995.

Hammerback, John C., and Richard J. Jensen. "The Rhetorical Worlds of César Chávez and Reijes Tijerina." *The Western Journal of Speech Communication* 44 (1980): 166–176.

———. "Ethnic Heritage As Rhetorical Legacy: The Plan of Delano." *Quarterly Journal of Speech* 80 (1994): 53–70.

———. *The Rhetorical Career of César Chávez*. College Station, TX: Texas A&M UP, 1998.

———, and Jose Angel Gutierrez. "'No Revolution Without Poets': The Rhetoric of Rodolfo 'Corky' Gonzales." *A War of Words: Chicano Protest in the 1960s and 1970s*. Westport, CN: Greenwood, 1985. 53–80.

Hasian, Jr., Marouf, and Thomas K. Nakayama. "The Fictions of Racialized Identities." *Judgment Calls: Rhetoric, Politics, and Indeterminacy*. Eds. John M. Sloop and James P. McDaniel. Boulder: Westview, 1998. 182–195.

Hernandez, Marcarena. "Standards of Beauty: Physical Attractiveness and Ethnic Identity." *Latinolink* November 23, 1998. November 23, 1999; http://www.latinolink.com/news/1999/1116imag.htm.

Herrera, Andrea O'Reilly. *Remembering Cuba: Legacy of a Diaspora*. Austin, TX: U of Texas P, 2001.

Hill Collins, Patricia. *Black Feminist Thought: Knowledge, Consciousness, and the Politics of Empowerment*. New York: Routledge, 2000.

———. *From Black Power to Hip Hop: Racism, Nationalism, and Feminism*. Philadelphia, PA: Temple UP, 2006.

Holling, Michelle. "*El Simpatico* Boxer: Underpinning Masculinity With a Rhetoric of Familia in *Resurrection Blvd.*" *Western Journal of Communication* 70 (2006): 91–114.

———. "Forming Oppositional Social Concord to California's Proposition 187 and Squelching Social Discord in the Vernacular Space of CHICLE." *Communication and Critical/Cultural Studies* 3 (2006): 202–222.

Holman Jones, Stacy. "Autoethnography: Making the Personal Political." *The Sage Handbook of Qualitative Research* (3rd ed.). Eds. Norman K. Denzin and Yvonna C. Lincoln. Thousand Oaks, CA: Sage, 2005. 763–791.

Holthouse, David. "Ricky-Ticky-Tacky." *The Phoenix New Times* December 1, 1999: 6.

hooks, bell. "Eating the Other: Desire and Resistance." *Black Looks: Race and Representation*. Boston, MA: South End, 1992. 21–39.

Inda, Jonathan A. "Performativity, materiality, and the racial body." *Latino Studies Journal* 11 (2000) 3: 74–99.

Ives, Brian. "Ricky Martin Urges President Clinton to Halt Bombing Practice." MTV.COM November 11, 1999. March 3, 2000; http://www.mtv.com/news/gallery/r/rmartin99110.html.

James, Mark, and El Vez. "Immigration Time." Perf. El Vez. *Grasiasland*. Sympathy For the Record Industry, 1994.

Jennings, Derek M. "Black, Brown and Green: The Shifting Landscape of Race and Economics in the Triangle." *The Independent Weekly* September 5, 2002; www.indyweek.com/durham/2001-7–11/cover2.html 11 July 2001.

Jensen, Richard J., and John C. Hammerback. "Radical Nationalism Among Chicanos: The Rhetoric of Jose Angel Gutierrez." *The Western Journal of Speech Communication* 44 (1982): 72–91.

Johnson, Kevin R. *How Did You Get to Be Mexican: A White/Brown Man's Search for Identity*. Philadelphia: Temple UP, 1999.

Jones, Steve. "Spanish-Spiced Hip-Hop." *USA Today* August 5, 2005. E1.

Keller, Gary D. *Hispanics and the United States Film: An Overview and Handbook*. Tempe, AZ: Bilingual Review, 1994.

Kramarae, Cheris. "Harassment and Everyday Life." *Women Making Meaning*. Ed. Lana F. Rakow. New York and London: Routledge, 1992. 100–120.

Krauss, C. "A Historic Figure Is Still Hated by Many in Mexico." *New York Times*, May 7, 2002. 1997; www.emayzine.com/lectures/la.htm.

Kuftinec, Sonja. "[Walking Through A] Ghost Town: Cultural Hauntologie in Mostar, Bosnia-Herzegovina or Mostar: A Performance Review." *Text and Performance Quarterly* 18 (1998): 81–95.

Lancaster, Roger N. "Guto's Performance: Notes on the Transvestism of Everyday Life." *Sex and Sexuality in Latin America*. Eds. Daniel Balderston and Donald J. Guy. New York: New York UP, 1997. 9–32.

Langellier, Kristin. "Voiceless Bodies, Bodiless Voices: The Future of Personal Narrative Performance." *The Future of Performance Studies: Visions and Revisions*. Ed. Sheron J. Dailey. Annandale, VA: National Communication Association, 1998. 207–213.

Latinos in North Carolina—some facts. *New South Productions*. Retrieved January 7, 2004, from http://www.newsouthproductions.com/info.htm.

LaWare, Margaret R. "Encountering Visions of Aztlan: Arguments for Ethnic Pride, Community Activism and Cultural Revitalization in Chicano Murals." *Argumentation and Advocacy* 34 (1998): 140–153.

Lawrence-Lightfoot, Sarah. *Respect: An Exploration*. New York: Perseus, 2000.

Limón, Jose. E. *American Encounters: Greater Mexico, the United States, and the Erotics of Culture*. Boston, MA: Beacon, 1998.

Lopez, Ana M. "Of Rhythms and Borders." *Everynight Life: Culture and Dance in Latin/o America*. Eds. Celeste Fraser Delgado and José Esteban Muñoz. Durham: Duke, 1991. 310–344.

Love, Lisa L., and Nathaniel Kohn. "This, That, and the Other: Fraught Possibilities of the Souvenir." *Text and Performance Quarterly* 21 (2001): 1–17.

Madison, D. Soyini. "Story, History, and Performance: Interpreting Oral History Through Black Performance Traditions." *Black Sacred Music: A Journal of Theomusicology* 8 (1994): 43–63.

————. "Performance, Personal Narratives, and the Politics of Possibility." *The Future of Performance Studies: Visions and Revisions.* Ed. Sheron J. Dailey. Annandale, VA: National Communication Association, 1998. 276–286.

————. "That Was My Occupation: Oral Narrative, Performance, and Black Feminist Thought." *Exceptional Spaces: Essays in Performance and History.* Ed. Della Pollock. Durham, NC: U of North Carolina P, 1998. 319–347.

————. "The Dialogic Performative in Critical Ethnography." *Text and Performance Quarterly* 26 (2006): 320–324.

————, and Judith Hamera. "Performance Studies at the Intersections." *The Sage Handbook of Performance Studies.* Eds. D. Soyini Madison and Judith Hamera. Thousand Oaks, CA: Sage, 2006. xi–xxv.

Martin, Jon B., and Gust A. Yep. "Eminem in Mainstream Public Discourse: Whiteness and the Appropriation of Black Masculinity." *Race/Gender/Media: Considering Diversity Across Audiences, Content, and Producers.* Ed. Rebecca Ann Lind. Boston, MA: Pearson, 2004. 228–235.

Martinez, Jacqueline M. *Phenomenology of Chicana Experience and Identity: Communication and Transformation in Praxis.* Lantham, MD: Rowman & Littlefield, 2000.

McGee, Michael Calvin. "The 'Ideograph': A Link Between Rhetoric and Ideology." *Quarterly Journal of Speech* 66 (1980): 1–16.

Menchaca, Denise. "Body and Soul: Performed Spiritual Enfleshment of Chicana Identity." *Kalediscope: An SCO Journal of Graduate Student Research* 1 (2002): 37–49.

Mirandé, Alfredo. *Hombres y Machos: Masculinity and Latino Culture.* Boulder: Westview, 1997.

Miserandino, Dominick A. "Interview With El Vez." *The Celebrity Café.* April 3, 1998. November 11, 2001; http://www.thecelebritycafe.com/interviews/el_vez.html.

Mohanty, Chandra Talpade. *Feminism Without Borders: Decolonizing Theory, Practicing Solidarity.* Durham, NC: Duke UP, 2003.

Moon, Dreama. "'Passing' As an Inter/cultural Discourse." *Readings in Cultural Contexts.* Eds. Judith N. Martin, Thomas K. Nakayama, and Lisa A. Flores. Mountain View: Mayfield, 1998. 322–330.

Mora, Pat. "Elena." *Making Face, Making Soul: Haciendo Caras.* Ed. Gloria Anzaldúa. San Francisco, CA: Aunt Lute, 1990. 193.

————. "Nepantla: Essays From the Land in the Middle." *Chicana Feminist Thought: The Basic Historical Writings.* Ed. Alma M. Garcia. New York: Routledge, 1997. 292–294.

Moraga, Cherríe. *The Last Generation: Prose and Poetry.* Boston, MA: South End, 1993.

————. *Loving in the War Years: Lo Que Nunca Paso Por Sus Labios* (2nd ed.). Cambridge, MA: South End, 2000.

————, and Gloria Anzaldúa. Eds. *This Bridge Called My Back: Writings By Radical Women of Color.* New York: Kitchen Table, 1981.

Moreman, Shane. "*Chupa Mi Cacahuate:* The Terms of My Latino Identity." *Studies in Symbolic Interaction, A Research Annual Volume 22.* Ed. Norman K. Denzin. Greenwich, CT: JAI Press, 1999. 65–75.

————. "Hybrid Performativity North and South of the Border: Traversing the Genres and Disciplines of Identity With Globalized Popular Culture." *Latino Communication Studies Today.* Ed. Angharad Valdivia. Peter Lang. In Press.

Moya, Paula. *Learning From Experience: Minority Identities, Multicultural Struggles.* Berkely, CA: U of California P, 2002.

Muñoz, Elías Miguel. *The Greatest Performance.* Houston: Arte Publico, 1991.

Muñoz, José Esteban. *Disidentifications: Queers of Color and the Performance of Politics.* Minneapolis: U of Minnesota P, 1999.

———. "Memory Performance: Luis Alfaro's 'Cuerpo Politizado.'" *Corpus Delecti: Performance Art of the Americas.* Ed. Coco Fusco. London: Routledge, 2000. 97–113.

———. "Feeling Brown: Ethnicity and Affect in Richard Bracho's *The Sweetest Hangover (and STDs).*" *Theatre Journal* 52 (2000): 67–79.

Nakayama, Thomas K. "Show/down Time: 'Race,' Gender, Sexuality, and Popular Culture." *Critical Studies in Mass Communication* 8 (1994): 162–179.

———. "Dis/orienting Identities: Asian Americans, History, and Intercultural Communication." *Our Voices: Essays in Culture, Ethnicity, and Communication* (3rd ed.). Eds. Alberto González, Marsha Houston, and Victoria Chen. Los Angeles, CA: Roxbury, 2000. 13–18.

Negrón-Muntaner, Frances. *Boricua Pop: Puerto Ricans and the Latinization of American Culture.* New York: NYU, 2004.

1999 Billboard Music Awards. FOX.

Noble, John. *Lonely Planet: Mexico City.* Melbourne: Lonely Planet, 1998.

Ono, Kent A. "A Letter/Essay I've Been Longing to Write in My Personal/Academic Voice." *Western Journal of Communication* 61 (1997): 114–125.

———, and John M. Sloop. "The Critique of Vernacular Discourse." *Communication Monographs* 62 (1995): 19–46.

———. *Shifting Borders: Rhetoric, Immigration, and California's Proposition 187.* Philadelphia, PA: Temple UP, 2002.

"Overview: Biography: Elvisology." *Elvis.com.* December 6, 2001. http://www.elvis.com/elvisology/bio/elvis_overview.asp.

Paz, Octavio. *The Labyrinth of Solitude: Life and Thought in Mexico.* Trans. Lysander Kemp. New York: Grove, 1961.

Pellegrini, Frank. "America Goes *Mucho Loco* for Ricky." *Time.com* May 13, 1999. March 2, 2000; http://www.time.com/time/daily/0,2960,24750/101990513,00.html.

Pérez, Emma. *The Decolonial Imaginary: Writing Chicanas Into History.* Bloomington, IN: Indiana UP, 1999.

Phelan, Peggy. *Unmarked: The Politics of Performance.* London: Routledge, 1993.

Píedra, José. "Hip Poetics." *Everynight Life: Culture and Dance in Latin/o America.* Eds. Celeste Fraser Delgado and José Esteban Muñoz. Durham: Duke UP, 1991. 93–140.

Pina, Michael. "The Archaic, Historical and Mythicized Dimensions of Aztlán." *Aztlán: Essays on the Chicano Homeland.* Eds. Rudolfo A. Anaya and Francisco Lomelí. Albuquerque, NM: El Norte, 1989. 14–48.

Piper, Adrian. "Passing for White, Passing for Black." *Passing and the Fictions of Identity.* Ed. Elaine K. Ginsberg. Durham, NC: Duke UP, 1996. 234–269.

———. "Xenophobioa and the Indexical Present II: Lecture." *Radical Street Performance: An International Anthology.* Ed. Jan Cohen-Cruz. New York: Routledge, 1998. 125–132.

Pollock, Della. *Telling Bodies, Performing Birth.* New York: Columbia UP, 1999.

———. "Marking New Directions in Performance Ethnography." *Text and Performance Quarterly* 26 (2006): 325–329.

Pough, Gwendolyn D. *Check It While I Wreck It: Black Womanhood, Hip-Hop Culture, and the Public Sphere.* Boston, MA: Northeastern UP, 2004.

Purnell, Kim L. "Listening to Lady Day: An Exploration of the Creative (Re)Negotiation of Identity Revealed in the Life Narratives and Music Lyrics of Billie Holiday." *Communication Quarterly* 50. 3/4 (2002): 444–466.

Raso, Anne M. *Ricky Martin: A Scrapbook in Words and Pictures.* New York: Bantam Doubleday, 1999.

Reid, Shaheem. "Reggaeton Star Don Omar Out to Spread Latino Unity." *MTV News* May 5, 2006. Retrieved September 4, 2006, from www.mtv.com/news/articles/1530242/05042006/omar_don.jhtml.

Ricky Martin: For One Night Only. CBS November 1999.

"Ricky Martin to Ask Clinton to Withdraw Navy From Vieques." *Latinolink* Oct.ober 29, 1999. December 8, 1999; http://www.latinolink.com/news/1999/1029rick.htm.

Rinderle, Susana. "*Quiénes Son/Quiénes Somos:* A Critical Analysis of the Changing Names for People of Mexican Descent Across History." *International and Intercultural Communication Annual: The Same But Different: Acknowledging the Diversity Within and Between Cultural Groups Vol. XXIX.* Eds. Mark P. Orbe, Brenda J. Allen, and Lisa A. Flores. Thousand Oaks, CA: Sage, 2006. 143–165.

Rivera, Raquel Z. *New York Ricans From the Hip Hop Zone.* New York: Palgrave, 2003.

Rodriguez, Amardo. "Culture to Culturing: Re-Imaging Our Understanding of Intercultural Relations." *Journal of Intercultural Communication* 5 (2002), Retrieved from http://www.immi.se/intercultural/.

Rodriguez, Cindy. "Ricky's Only One Star in a Huge Latin Galaxy." *Latinolink* August 9, 1999. December 8, 1999; http://www.latinolink.com/commentary/1999/0809rick.htm.

Rodriguez, Clara E. *Heroes, Lovers, and Others: The Story of Latinos in Hollywood.* Washington D.C.: Smithsonian Books, 2004.

Rodríguez, Juana María. *Queer Latinidad: Identity Practices, Discursive Spaces.* New York: New York UP, 2003.

Rodriguez-Dominguez, Victor M. "Is Ricky Martin Really a Puerto Rican (Latino) Phenomenon?" *Latinolink* May 20, 1999. December 8, 1999; http://www.latinolink.com/opinion/opinion99/0520oric.htm.

Rosa, Robi, and Desmond Child. "Livin' la Vida Loca." Perf. Ricky Martin. *Ricky Martin.* Columbia, 1999.

———, and George Noriega. "Shake Your Bon Bon." Perf. Ricky Martin. *Ricky Martin.* Columbia, 1999.

———, George Noriega, and Jon Secada. "She's All I Ever Had." Perf. Ricky Martin. *Ricky Martin.* Columbia, 1999.

Ruiz, Manual Alejandro. "Reggaeton Latino (Chosen Few Remix)." Perf. Don Omar, Fat Joe, N.O.R.E., and LDA. *Don Omar: Da Hitman Reggaeton Latino.* Universal, 2005.

Said, Edward. *Orientalism.* New York: Vintage, 1979.

Saldívar, José David. *Border Matters: Remapping American Cultural Studies.* Berkeley, CA: U of California P, 1997.

Sánchez, Rosaura. "On a Critical Realist Theory of Identity." *Identity Politics Reconsidered.* Eds. Linda Martín Alcoff, Michael Hames-García, Satya P. Mohanty, and Paula M.L. Moya. New York: Palgrave, 2006. 31–52.

Sandoval, Chela. *Methodology of the Oppressed.* Minneapolis, MN: U of Minnesota P, 2000.

Sandoval-Sánchez, Alberto. *José Can You See?: Latinos On and Off Broadway.* Madison, WI: U of Wisconsin P, 1999.

———, and Nancy Saporta Sternbach. *Stages of Life: Transcultural Performance and Identity in U.S. Latina Theater.* Tucson, AZ: U of Arizona P, 2001.

Santiago, Victor. "Oye Mi Canto." Perf. N.O.R.E., Daddy Yankee, Nina Sky, Big Mato, and Gem Star. *Oye Mi Canto.* Def Jam, 2004.

Schechner, Richard. *Performance Studies: An Introduction*. New York: Routledge, 2002.

Scheerer, Mark. "Ricky Martin Leading the Latin (Music) Revolution." *CNN.COM* May 18, 1999. February 2, 2000; http://www.cnn.com/SHOWBIZ/MUSIC/9905/17/latin/music.

Scott, James C. *Domination and the Arts of Resistance: Hidden Transcripts*. New Haven: Yale UP, 1990.

Sedano, Michael Victor. "Chicanismo: A Rhetorical Analysis of Themes and Images of Selected Poetry From the Chicano Movement." *The Western Journal of Speech Communication* 44 (1980): 177–190.

Sedgwick, Eve Kosofsky. *Tendencies*. Durham, NC: Duke UP, 1993.

Serros, Michele. *Chicana Falsa and Other Stories of Death, Identity, and Oxnard*. New York: Riverhead, 1993.

Shome, Raka. "Postcolonial Interventions in the Rhetorical Canon: An 'Other' View." *Contemporary Rhetorical Theory*. Eds. John Lucaites, Celeste Condit, and Sally Caudill. New York: Guilford, 1998. 591–608.

Shugart, Helene A. "Performing Ambiguity: The Passing of Ellen DeGeneres." *Text and Performance Quarterly* 23 (2003): 30–54.

Sinfield, Alan. "Diaspora and Hybridity: Queer Identities and Ethnicity Model." *Textual Practice* 10 (1996): 271–293.

Sloop, John M. "'Apology Made to Whoever Pleases': Cultural Discipline and the Grounds of Interpretation." *Communication Quarterly* 42 (1994): 345–362.

Stavans, Ilán. "The Latin Phallus." *The Latino Studies Reader: Culture, Economy, and Society*. Eds. Antonia Darder and Rodolfo D Torres. Malden, MA: Blackwell Publishers, 1998. 228–239.

Tafolla, Carmen. "La Malinche." *Infinite Divisions: An Anthology of Chicana Literature*. Eds. Tey Diana Rebolledo and Eliana S. Rivero. Tucson, AZ: U of Arizona P, 1993. 198–199.

Tanno, Dolores V. "Names, Narratives, and the Evolution of Ethnic Identity." *Our Voices: Essays in Culture, Ethnicity, and Communication*. Eds. Alberto González, Marsha Houston, and Victoria Chen. (2nd ed.). Los Angeles: Roxbury, 2000. 25–28.

Taylor, Diana. "Making a Spectacle: The Mothers of the Plaza de Mayo." *Radical Street Performance: An International Anthology*. Ed. Jan Cohen-Cruz. New York: Routledge, 1998. 74–85.

———. *The Archive and the Repertoire: Performing Cultural Memory in the Americas*. Durham, NC: Duke University P, 2003.

The Barbara Walters Special. ABC. March 2000.

The Chosen Few. Director and Producer Manuel Alejandor Ruiz. *The Chosen Few: El Documental*. 2005.

Thigpen, David E. "Spicing the Mix: Latin Pop Prepares to Take on America." *Time* March 15, 1999: 80.

Torres-Saillant, Silvio. "Inventing the Race: Latinos and the Ethnoracial Pentagon." *Latino Studies* 1 (2003): 123–151.

Troyano, Alina. *I, Carmelita Tropicana: Performing Between Cultures*. Boston: Beacon, 2000.

Turner, Terence S. "The Social Skin." *Reading the Social Body*. Eds. Catherine B. Burroughs and Jeffrey David Ehrenreich. Iowa City: U of Iowa P, 1993. 15–39.

"V Day Top 10." *U Magazine*. Feb. 2000: 12–13.

Valdivia, Angharad. *A Latina in the Land of Hollywood and Other Essays on Media Culture*. Tucson, AZ: U of Arizona P, 2000.

———. Latinas As Radical Hybrid: "Transnationally Gendered Traces in Mainstream Media." *Global Media Journal* 3 (2004): 1–21.

Walker, Marguerite. "Border *Boda* or Divorce *Fronterizo?" Radical Street Performance: An International Anthology.* Ed. Jan Cohen-Cruz. New York: Routledge, 1998. 86–89.

Watrous, Peter. "Latin Musicians Discover New Worlds to Conquer." *Latinolink* May 23, 1999. December 8, 1999; http://www.latinolink.com/art/art99/0523amus.htm.

Weider, Judy. "All the Way Out: George Michael." *The Advocate.* January 19, 1999: 24–41.

Willis, Jennifer L. "'Latino Night': Performances of Latino/a Culture in Northwest Ohio." *Communication Quarterly* 45 (1997): 335–354.

———, and Alberto González. "Reconceptualizing Gender Through Dialogue: The Case of the Tex-Mex Madonna." *Women and Language* 20 (1997): 9–12.

Wolk, Josh. "La Vida Vota. " *Entertainment Weekly Online* November 1, 1999. March 2, 2000; http://www.ew.com/ew/daily/0,2514,2169,rickymartinwillmeet.html.

Zimmerman, Marc. "Erasure, Imposition and Crossover of Puerto Ricans and Chicanos in U.S. Film and Music Culture." *Latino Studies* 1 (2003): 115–122.

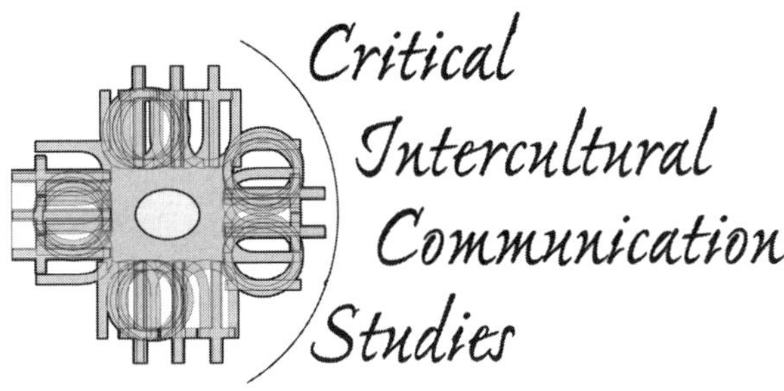

General Editor, Thomas K. Nakayama

Critical approaches to the study of intercultural communication have arisen at the end of the twentieth century and are poised to flourish in the new millenium. As cultures come into contact—driven by migration, refugees, the internet, wars, media, transnational capitalism, cultural imperialism, and more—critical interrogations of the ways that cultures interact communicatively are needed to understand culture and communication. This series will interrogate—from a critical perspective—the role of communication in intercultural contact, in both domestic and international contexts. This series is open to studies in key areas such as postcolonialism, transnationalism, critical race theory, queer diaspora studies, and critical feminist approaches as they relate to intercultural communication, tuning into the complexities of power relations in intercultural communication. Proposals might focus on various contexts of intercultural communication such as international advertising, popular culture, language policies, hate crimes, ethnic cleansing and ethnic group conflicts, as well as engaging theoretical issues such as hybridity, displacement, multiplicity, identity, orientalism, and materialism. By creating a space for these critical approaches, this series will be at the forefront of this new wave in intercultural communication scholarship. Manuscripts and proposals are welcome that advance this new approach.

For additional information about this series or for the submission of manuscripts, please contact:

> Dr. Thomas K. Nakayama
> Hugh Downs School of Human Communication
> Arizona State University
> P.O. Box 871205
> Tempe, AZ 85287-1205

To order other books in this series, please contact our Customer Service Department:
> (800) 770-LANG (within the U.S.)
> (212) 647-7706 (outside the U.S.)
> (212) 647-7707 FAX

Or browse online by series:
> www.peterlang.com